Far
Beyond
the Field

Translations from the Asian Classics

Translations from the Asian Classics

Editorial Board

Wm. Theodore de Bary, Chair

Paul Anderer

Irene Bloom

Donald Keene

George A. Saliba

Haruo Shirane

David D. W. Wang

Burton Watson

Far Beyond the Field

Haiku by Japanese Women

An Anthology

*Compiled, Translated, and
with an Introduction by*
MAKOTO UEDA

*Columbia
University
Press
New York*

Columbia University Press
Publishers Since 1893
New York   Chichester, West Sussex

© 2003 Columbia University Press
All rights reserved

Library of Congress Cataloging-in-Publication Data
Far beyond the field : haiku by Japanese women : an anthology /
  compiled, translated, and with an introduction by Makoto Ueda.
     p. cm.—(Translations from the Asian classics)
   Includes bibliographical references.
   ISBN 978-0-231-12862-9 (cloth)   —ISBN 978-0-231-12863-6
(paper)
   1. Haiku—Translations into English.   2. Japanese poetry—
Women authors—Translations into English.   I. Title: Haiku by
Japanese women.   II. Ueda, Makoto, 1931–   III. Series.

PL 782.E3 F37 2003
895.6'1041089287—dc21

                                                       2002034832

Contents

Preface ix

Introduction xiii

Den Sutejo (1633–1698) 1

Kawai Chigetsu (1634?–1718) 13

Shiba Sonome (1664–1726) 25

Chiyojo (1703–1775) 37

Enomoto Seifu (1732–1815) 49

Tagami Kikusha (1753–1826) 61

Takeshita Shizunojo (1887–1951) 73

Sugita Hisajo (1890–1946) 85

Hashimoto Takako (1899–1963) 97

Mitsuhashi Takajo (1899–1972) 109

Ishibashi Hideno (1909–1947) 121

Katsura Nobuko (b. 1914) 133

Yoshino Yoshiko (b. 1915) 145

Tsuda Kiyoko (b. 1920) 157

Inahata Teiko (b. 1931) 169

Uda Kiyoko (b. 1935) 181

Kuroda Momoko (b. 1938) 193

Tsuji Momoko (b. 1945) 205

Katayama Yumiko (b. 1952) 217

Mayuzumi Madoka (b. 1965) 229

Selected Bibliography 241

Far
Beyond
the Field

Preface

This is a collection of four hundred haiku written by twenty Japanese women poets over a period of three and one-half centuries. I have selected poets from different eras in the history of haiku so that the reader may get an overview of the way in which this seventeen-syllable form succeeded in establishing itself from the earliest times to the present. The finest work done by a female haiku poet exemplifies her era just as well as that of a male poet, even though her status in her time's haiku circles may not have been very high. Compared with haiku written by men, the world of women's haiku is just as rich and colorful, and slightly more lyrical and erotic. Because haiku traditionally tended to shun strong passion and romantic love, to explore those areas was to go counter to established tradition, yet some women poets consciously or subconsciously did so, thereby helping to expand the world of haiku.

It was difficult to select women poets for this anthology: there were too few of them in premodern times, and there are too many today. Before the twentieth century, haiku was mostly considered a male preserve; women were expected to write *tanka*, a more elegant and lyrical literary genre. Few collections of haiku by premodern female poets are readily available today, not only because such poets were few in number but because most haiku scholars and anthologists in today's Japan are male. On the other hand, it has been estimated that women constitute some 70 percent of the haiku-writing population in Japan at the present time. *Hototogisu* (The mountain cuckoo), the most prestigious and longest-lasting haiku magazine, has a woman for its chief editor. I could have easily compiled an anthology of haiku written by twenty, thirty, or forty contemporary women poets. However, I felt it more important to show the entire tradition of women's haiku in Japan, for that tradition has been long, rich, and largely unknown to the Western world. I also wanted to give some sense of each poet's individual style, and to do so in fewer than twenty poems seemed very difficult indeed.

As is obvious by now, I am using the term *haiku* to denote all serious poems written in the seventeen-syllable form since the sixteenth century. Such poems were called *hokku* before the twentieth century, but since this anthology covers both modern and premodern times I wanted to avoid the confusion of mutiple names. Similarly, the term *tanka* includes all poems composed with the 5-7-5-7-7 syllable pattern, regardless of the period they come from. *Haikai*, as used in this book, designates all literary products written in the spirit of haiku, including haiku, *renku* (linked verse), and *haibun* (haiku prose). All Japanese names appear in the Japanese order, the surname preceding the given name or *haigō* (haiku name), except when the poets are authors of books in English. I have also followed the Japanese custom of calling the poet by her *haigō* or by her given name when the full name is not used. Prior to 1873 the Japanese used the lunar calendar, but again for the sake of uniformity I have converted all dates into their Gregorian equivalents.

The poets are presented in chronological order. I have tried to do the same for the poems; however, because of the lack of biographical material, it was difficult to do so for the work of the premodern poets. In their case the arrangement is largely based on my guesswork, with no hard evidence. It is hoped that as studies on those poets progress, their poems will be dated with more scholarly authority. Kinuko Jambor, in her recent book on Shiba

Sonome, has already shown the way. Haiku by modern poets are less difficult to date, but because many of them were published in collections without exact dates, I have often had to make an educated guess, and I am certain I have erred from time to time. The poems appear in the original Japanese in the lower margin of each page. The citation in the following parentheses refers to the place where the original haiku can be found (see the Selected Bibliography for details).

Eleven of the authors hold copyrights, and I am happy to say they kindly granted me permission to translate and publish their poems here. My thanks are due to Hashimoto Miyoko (for Hashimoto Takako), Mitsuhashi Yōichi (for Mitsuhashi Takajo), Katsura Nobuko, Yoshino Yoshiko, Tsuda Kiyoko, Inahata Teiko, Uda Kiyoko, Kuroda Momoko, Tsuji Momoko, Katayama Yumiko, and Mayuzumi Madoka. I am also grateful to the Hoover Institution Library at Stanford University, the library at the Harvard-Yenching Institute, and the University of Michigan East Asiatic Library for the materials I have used. Mr. J. M. B. Edwards carefully read the entire manuscript and gave me numerous suggestions for improving it; while I was unable to follow all of them, I know the book gained a great deal from his help. Two anonymous readers for Columbia University Press provided me with a series of recommendations that only experts in the field could offer; accordingly, I have tried to remedy any inadequacies. Nevertheless, all the errors and infelicities that may be found in the book are mine.

Introduction

R. H. Blyth, although he contributed more than anyone to an international understanding of haiku, once wrote that he doubted whether women could write in the seventeen-syllable form: "Haiku poetesses," he said, "are only fifth class."[1] While the magisterial phrasing is characteristic of Blyth, the view itself merely echoes a centuries-old Japanese bias. How old—and prevalent—that bias was can be seen from a precept attributed to Matsuo Bashō (1644–1694): "Never befriend a woman who writes haiku. Don't take her either as a teacher or as a student. . . . In general, men should associate with women only for the sake of securing an heir."[2] Certainly the attribution is wrong, for Bashō, the most prestigious of the haiku masters, not only associated with female poets but took several of them under his wing. He even had their verses published in the anthologies of his haiku group. Still, that the precept was widely believed to be his is itself clear evidence of a prevailing sexual prejudice in haiku circles of the seventeenth and eighteenth centuries.

The prejudice lingered well into the twentieth century. For instance, when a certain young woman once visited the eminent haiku poet Katō Shūson (1905–1993) and asked if she could be allowed to join his haiku group, he replied: "Instead of writing haiku or doing anything else, a young lady like you should try to get happily married.

[1] Blyth, A *History of Haiku*, 1:34.
[2] Cited in Kawashima, *Joryū haijin*, 6.

Find a husband, struggle with pots and pans in the kitchen, have children. Giving birth to haiku after going through all that—why, those would be true haiku."[3] To be fair to Shūson, he was one of the so-called humanist haiku poets who emphasized the importance of spiritual and moral discipline for anyone interested in writing poetry. Also, his comment does not completely shut the door on women who want to write haiku; as a matter of fact, his wife Chiyoko was a haiku poet. Yet it is undeniable that beneath the comment lay the traditional patriarchal attitude: a woman should first be a good wife and mother, and writing haiku or doing anything else should be subordinate to the performance of that role.

In today's Japan, where more women than men write haiku, such an attitude is generally considered an anachronism. Indeed, a number of haiku groups, each publishing a magazine, are currently headed by women. For women haiku poets to have come this far, however, they have had to tread a long and rough road over many generations. Given the feudalistic nature of premodern Japanese society, that is true of all the traditional literary genres. But women haiku poets have probably suffered the most because from its very beginning haiku was regarded as a male literary genre.

Women in the Formative Years of Haiku

Historical factors, especially the availability of *tanka* as an alternative form of poetic expression, account for haiku being considered a male preserve. Long before *renku*, the parent of haiku, made its appearance on the Japanese poetic scene, *tanka* had established itself as the central and most revered of all literary genres. Those who had helped

---

[3] Cited in Nakajima Hideko, "Sengo joryū haiku gairon," in *Gendai shiika shū*, vol. 24, *Josei sakka shiriizu*, ed. Nakamura et al., 160.

to perfect this thirty-one-syllable verse form were the talented noblewomen who served at the imperial court in the ninth and tenth centuries, when male courtiers were writing poetry largely in Chinese. To be sure, noblemen did compose *tanka* too, but usually they did so when they exchanged poems with court ladies. As a consequence, the aesthetics of *tanka* came to be deeply feminine, prizing elegance, delicacy, and a high degree of refinement. Those ideals were inherited, with some modifications, by later *tanka* poets, most of whom were male. Similar ideals became the aims of *renga*, too, when it arose during the fourteenth and fifteenth centuries. There were hardly any noblewomen who participated in *renga*, even though their typical sensibilities informed it. Then a reaction came with the rise of *renku* in the sixteenth century, gradually appealing to a more popular level of society. That segment consisted almost exclusively of male poets, inasmuch as the aesthetic ideals of *renku* were intended to be antithetical to the feminine sensibilities that permeated *tanka*. Women, who had been distanced by *renga*, were even farther away from *renku*. For *renku*, and its offspring haiku, were considered too inelegant for a lady to try her hand at; after all, if she wanted to write a poem, she had the graceful, highly respected *tanka* form readily available.

Another major factor that prevented women from writing haiku was more social. Whereas *tanka* was usually composed by a poet in solitude, the composition of *renku* and haiku was part of a group activity. In writing linked poetry in the lighthearted (that is, *haikai*) style, poets who made up the team were seated in the same room and contributed stanzas in turn. In writing haiku, too, poets would hold what are now known as *kukai* (haiku-writing parties), where they composed seventeen-syllable verses on the same topic. Given the sexual biases of Japanese society at the time, it was difficult for a woman to join the men on such occasions. Indeed, a Confucian dictum then prevalent taught that boys and girls were not to sit together after reaching the seventh year. Women were expected to serve food and drink to the guests, but not to participate in the poetic activities that went on in the room.

It is no wonder, then, that there were few female poets in the earliest years of haiku. The two oldest anthologies of haiku and *renku*, *Chikuba kyōginshū* (Mad verse of youth, 1499) and *Inu tsukuba shū* (The dog Tsukuba collection, 1514), do not ascribe authorship, but it is highly unlikely that they include any work by women, for they are loaded with coarse, crude, even obscene verses. The earliest documentary evidence for female authorship of *haikai* is dated more than a century later. *Enoko shū* (The puppy collection, 1633), which collected verses written by poets of Teimon, the oldest school of *haikai*, contains works by a person identified only as "Mitsusada's wife." Of the 178 poets represented in the anthology, she was the lone woman. That statistic, and her being listed under her husband's name, suggest the kind of status to which women were confined in haiku circles during this seminal period.

Be that as it may, women had begun writing haiku by the early seventeenth century, and there was a reason for it: compared with the earliest writers of haiku and *renku*, poets of the Teimon school depended more on wit, classical allusion, and wordplay for humor than on scatological or pornographic references, thereby making it easier for a lady to write in that genre. As the Teimon school came to dominate the *haikai* scene in the mid-seventeenth century, more women started composing haiku and *renku*. *Yumemigusa* (Dreaming grass, 1656) has 3 women among its 511 contributors; *Gyokukai shū* (The collection from the sea, 1656) numbers 13 among its 658. *Zoku yamanoi* (A sequel to *The mountain well*, 1667), one of the largest collections of Teimon verse, includes 15 women among 967 poets. Those figures show that the increase was slow but steady.

By 1684, there had emerged a sufficient number of female haiku poets to enable Ihara Saikaku (1642–1693), a renowned writer of fiction as well as *haikai*, to compile

Haikai nyokasen (Thirty-six *haikai* poetesses), a book comprising thirty-six haiku written by thirty-six women poets, each poem accompanied by a portrait of the author and a brief comment on her. In his preface Saikaku wrote: "Haiku, being part of Japanese poetry, is one of the refined arts suitable for women to learn.... Therefore, even a female stable hand in a remote village would have the heart to avoid cutting blooming boughs for firewood, feel sorry for marring the new snow in her vegetable garden with footprints, be moved by the sunrise and sunset glows seen through the window of her mountain hut, and write a haiku by imagining famous places in poetry like the Sea of Nago."[4] Even when allowance is made for Saikaku's rhetoric, one can detect the popularity of haiku beginning to spread to all classes of women. Among the thirty-six poets selected by Saikaku, eleven lived in rural areas. Of the others, four were courtesans, three were chambermaids, another three were nuns, and one was a concubine.

Saikaku compiled the illustrated anthology more out of his interest in women than out of respect for their poetry. By and large, the *haikai* masters who were his contemporaries remained inattentive to women's haiku. If there was one exception, it would be the recognition of Den Sutejo (1633–1698) whose verse is found in several *haikai* anthologies published in the 1660s. Her haiku do not show much originality, but her wit as well as her command of rhetorical devices are not inferior to those of male poets in the Teimon school. *Zoku yamanoi* contains thirty-five haiku and five *renku* verses by her. It appears that she was considered a more accomplished poet than her husband, for the latter had only eleven haiku accepted in the same anthology. Incidentally, the book also includes twenty-eight haiku and three linked verses written by the young

---

[4] Ebara et al., eds., *Teihon Saikaku zenshū*, vol. 11, part 1, 463. The Sea of Nago refers to a part of Osaka Bay often celebrated in classical *tanka*.

Bashō. In this respect, at least, it seems that Sutejo was the better known poet.

Bashō's Female Students

Bashō, however, soon parted ways with the Teimon school. After a period of experiment, he came, in the late 1680s, to establish his own style of haiku, a style that was to exert immense influence over poets of the succeeding centuries. To put it briefly, he transformed haiku from a mere sportive verse into a mature form of poetry capable of embodying human experience at the deepest level. In the process of transformation he proposed two aesthetic ideals: *sabi* (loneliness), a forlorn beauty that results from the poet's absorption in the insentient universe; and *karumi* (lightness), a humorous poetic effect produced when the poet looks at human reality from a viewpoint that transcends it. Not a theorist by nature, Bashō revealed these ideals by commenting on his students' verses and by publishing *haikai* anthologies. His own poems in the anthologies and in his travel journals, such as *Oku no hosomichi* (The narrow road to the far north, 1689), also displayed what he was aiming at as a poet. Of the anthologies, *Sarumino* (The monkey's straw raincoat, 1691) best exemplified the ideal of *sabi*, and *Sumidawara* (The sack of charcoal, 1694) presented a number of haiku and *renku* that produce the effect of *karumi*.

Although Bashō in his later years had a great many followers all over Japan, female students who enjoyed his personal guidance numbered only a few. Of the 118 poets who contributed verses to *Sarumino*, just 5 were women; in *Sumidawara* the ratio was 2 out of 79. No doubt the paucity of women among his students had more to do with the contemporary social situation than with his personal views on gender. His attitude toward women students can be glimpsed, for instance, in a letter he sent from his residence in Edo (the modern Tokyo) to one such student in

Kyoto named Nozawa Ukō. Dated 3 March 1693, the letter reads in part: "People here who have read the headnote to your haiku in *Sarumino* think well of you, speculating what a beautiful and virtuous lady you must be. I tell them that you are not especially beautiful or virtuous but simply have a mind that understands the pathos of things. I hope you will discipline your mind further in this direction."[5] The haiku referred to is

> Because I am frail and prone to illness, it had not been easy for me even to do my hair. So I became a nun last spring.

combs, hairpins	kōgai mo
such are the things of the past—	kushi mo mukashi ya
a fallen camellia	chiritsubaki

Bashō's letter reveals that while his students in Edo made much of the fact that Ukō was a woman, he treated her as a poet above all and gave her exactly the same kind of advice he would have given a male student. Unfortunately, Ukō seems to have had to curtail her poetic activities shortly after, since she was in social disgrace when her husband Bonchō (d. 1714) was convicted of some crime (probably smuggling). He spent several years in prison, during which time Bashō passed away.

Aside from Ukō, two other women distinguished themselves among Bashō's students: Kawai Chigetsu (1634?–1718) and Shiba Sonome (1664–1726). Chigetsu seems to have been very close to Bashō in his later years. Whenever he came to the southern coast of Lake Biwa, she invited him to stay at her home, even building a new house for his visit in 1691. One of her letters to him suggests she took care of his laundry whenever he was in the area, whether he was staying with her or not. The grateful teacher returned the favor

---

[5] *Kokugo kokubun* 42, no. 6 (1973), 26.

in various ways, at one time giving her a handwritten copy of his *haibun*, and at another time inviting her to join the team that composed a *renku* for *Sarumino*. After he died, she remained in close contact with his other disciples and continued to write haiku in the style of the Bashō school.

Sonome became well known because in one of his most famous haiku Bashō compared her to a pure white chrysanthemum:

white chrysanthemum	*shiragiku no*
without a speck of dust	*me ni tatete miru*
the eyes can catch	*chiri mo nashi*

Bashō wrote the haiku to start off a *renku* composition at Sonome's house, so it goes without saying that the verse had salutational connotations. Still, he would not have addressed his hostess in such terms if she had been unattractive. Also, since the person who followed with the second verse was Sonome and not her husband, who was a poet too, her poetic talent must have been highly regarded by Bashō and his group. Indeed, she went on to become one of the first women who taught *haikai* professionally. While Chigetsu was more of a motherly patron who never promoted herself as a poet, Sonome was ambitious, independent, and daring. Perhaps because of that, a number of anecdotes, whether true or fictional, adorn her biographies. For example, it is said that although she was a housewife, she did not do the dishes after each meal but threw them into a large tub and left them soaking in the water for days, until she could take time off from her poetic activities.

Most other women poets of the Bashō school received poetic instruction less from Bashō than from his leading disciples. Deserving of mention here are Mukai Chine (d. 1688) and the nun Tagami (1645–1719), both of whom had their verses included in *Sarumino*; Kana, whose haiku appear in *Sumidawara*; Terasaki Shihaku (d. 1718?), the first female compiler of a *haikai* anthology; Nagano Rinjo (1674–1757), whose surviving verses number as many as 650; and Shūshiki (1669–1725), who lived in Edo and excelled in writing witty, urbane verses. In 1702 Bashō's disciple Ōta Hakusetsu (1661–1725) undertook to compile a collection of haiku by contemporary women poets; it was published as the second volume of *Haikai Mikawa Komachi* (*Haikai* verses by the followers of Komachi in Mikawa Province).[6] The collection comprised 103 haiku written by 66 women representing Mikawa (Aichi Prefecture) and many other provinces. Although most of the poets mentioned above are included, a great majority of the remainder were obscure women with plain names such as Kame, Kichi, and Hatsu. Indeed, Hakusetsu says in his preface that in compiling the anthology he collected verses of common townswomen at random, including courtesans and girls six or seven years old. Clearly since Saikaku's time, the practice of writing haiku had spread still further in various classes and kinds of women.

The Eighteenth and Nineteenth Centuries

During the first half of the eighteenth century, haiku and *renku* began a steady decline. One reason was the increased codification of the art of writing *haikai* verses: professional teachers, eager to impress their students, created more and more complicated rules of composition. Another and more important reason was Bashō's death in 1694. Many of his students, each claiming to be the legitimate heir to their prestigious teacher, went their separate ways, promoting one or another of what they claimed were his precepts. Perhaps the greatest culprit was Kagami Shikō

---

[6] Komachi was a ninth-century woman poet of legendary beauty and poetic talent.

(1665–1731) who, under the pretext of teaching the principle of *karumi*, advocated the use of familiar topics and simple language in verse writing, without stressing the importance of spiritual attainment. Since he was good at didactic writing, and since plain verse was easy to write, his school became extremely popular all over Japan, especially in the rural provinces.

It was unfortunate that the most famous of all women haiku poets in premodern Japan, Chiyojo (1703–1775), had to come under Shikō's influence because of the era she lived in. To make the situation worse, she met Shikō in person at the impressionable age of sixteen and began asking for his guidance soon after. Thus a large majority of her verses are written in the style of his school, often presenting stereotyped sentiments in banal diction. On the other hand, Shikō's extravagant praise brought her fame at a young age, which in turn enabled her to travel, associate with male poets, and devote herself to writing verse to an extent unimaginable for an ordinary woman of the time. And, with time and experience, she learned to apply her considerable gifts to observing the smallest workings of nature and finding exquisite beauty in them. She also acquired a sensuous appreciation of people and their problems, which had been rare in the previous haiku tradition.

A movement that attempted to break with the stagnant state of haiku arose in the second half of the eighteenth century and reaped a measure of success. Its leader, Yosa Buson (1716–1784), tried to elevate the level of contemporary poetry by promoting the principle of *rizoku* (detachment from the mundane); the poet, he insisted, should discover beauty in a sphere high above earthly reality. A number of poets, mainly in Kyoto and Osaka, who shared his poetic ideal gathered around him and formed a group, which grew larger with time. Few of its members, however, were women. Buson himself seems to have had little sexual bias. Once, when a certain woman and her daughter wanted to join his followers, Buson was overjoyed and said: "I have long regretted having no woman in my group."[7] Perhaps to get more women interested in haiku, he compiled a collection of verse by women that ended up becoming the best-known book of its kind in premodern Japan. Entitled *Tamamo shū* (The collection of watergrass) and published in 1774, it assembles 449 haiku written by 118 female poets, including many of those already referred to. What differentiates this book from the preceding two anthologies of women's haiku is, above all, the compiler's discriminating critical taste. Most of the haiku that appear in it are the authors' finest works, and the number of poems selected from each author corresponds appropriately to her stature in the history of haiku, even from today's vantage point.

For whatever reason, however, *Tamamo shū* excluded works of living poets. If the editorial policy had been more inclusive, Buson would surely have accepted some haiku from Chiyojo, who wrote the preface to the anthology, and from Taniguchi Denjo (d. 1779), a well-known *haikai* teacher in Edo who contributed the postscript. He might also have taken samples from the works of Shokyūni (1714–1781), the author of a poetic journal entitled *Shūfū-ki* (The journal of an autumn wind), and Kasen (1716?–1776), a courtesan legendary for her skills in many arts. Among other candidates for inclusion are those who best represent the two younger generations: Enomoto Seifu (1732–1814) and Tagami Kikusha (1753–1826).

Seifu is considered by some modern critics to be the greatest woman haiku poet of premodern Japan. A resident of a town near Edo, she does not seem to have come in direct contact with Buson's group, but like Buson she was well-read in classical literature and aspired to the poetic ideals that it embodied. Again like Buson, she was dissatisfied with much of the *haikai* poetry written in her

---

[7] Buson's letter is dated 7 February 1777. See Hisamatsu and Imoto, eds., *Koten haibungaku taikei*, 12:455.

time and wanted to learn directly from Bashō. The haiku she wrote on an anniversary of Bashō's death

I droop my head—	*fushite omou*
thoughts over the withered moor	*kareno no jō wo*
past and present	*ima mukashi*

alludes to Bashō's deathbed poem

on a journey, ill—	*tabi ni yande*
my dreams roam about	*yume wa kareno wo*
on a withered moor	*kakemeguru*

and suggests her dismay at the desolate poetic landscape in her own time. Distinctly apart from the majority of haiku produced by her contemporaries, her haiku are permeated with aspiration for a transcendent world of purity and solitude.

While Seifu approached Bashō through reading and contemplation, Kikusha tried to attain the same end by purposeful travel. Widowed at the age of twenty-three, she became a Buddhist nun and spent much of her remaining life wandering throughout Japan. Unfortunately, most of the poets she met on the road belonged to Shikō's school of haiku, and so her considerable poetic talent came to be molded into their style. On the other hand, at various places she became acquainted with experts in other arts, under whom she was able to polish her own skills in *tanka*, Chinese verse, calligraphy, painting, music, and the tea ceremony. Her book of poetry, *Taorigiku* (Plucked chrysanthemums, 1812), is not only illustrated with her own drawings but also has a sprinkling of poems in classical Chinese, each accompanied by a haiku written on the same topic.

The nineteenth century, except for its last ten years or so, was a dark age for haiku and for most other literary genres. With Japan largely isolated from the rest of the world, its poets had no cultural stimulation from the outside; internally, their creativity was effectively stifled by the oppressive institutions of feudal society. Writers of haiku, even someone with a character as strong as Kobayashi Issa (1763–1828), had to respect the established hierarchical system if they wanted to make a living as a professional *haikai* master. Because of the increased literacy rate, more women began to take up writing verse, either as a hobby or professionally, but most of their works offer nothing more than conventional wisdom or trite sentiments or commonplace observations in uninspiring language. The women poets worthy of mention in this period are just two: Igarashi Hamamo (1772–1848?), who compiled the first anthology of *renku* written exclusively by women; and Ichihara Tayo (1776–1865), who, despite living in a remote northeastern town, published a large collection of haiku that can be favorably compared to anything by her male contemporaries. A new era in the history of haiku did not dawn until the inflow of Western culture began toward the very end of the century.

The Struggle of the New in Early Modern Japan

The coming of the Meiji Restoration and Japan's new positive attitude toward importing Western culture soon affected all literature, and haiku was no exception. Beginning in the 1890s, the mannerism of the nineteenth-century haiku came under heavy attack, as a group of young poets refused to compose the seventeen-syllable verse on trite topics using a restricted vocabulary. Its leader, Masaoka Shiki (1867–1902), was determined to write revolutionary haiku in a *kukai*, or haiku-writing party, where old-fashioned topics would typically be treated in words sanctioned by tradition. His main aesthetic principle was *shasei* (sketch from life), which required the poet to go various places and copy things as he actually saw them. Shiki had many other innovative ideas, one of them being that more women should write haiku. He thought that compared with *tanka*, which traditionally dealt with elegant objects, haiku was lacking in pretension and so was more readily available to ordinary women. He praised five female poets of the past: Sutejo, Chigetsu, Sonome, Shūshiki, and Chiyojo. His life, however, was too short for him to do much to encourage women to write haiku.

His lead, however, was followed with great persistence by Takahama Kyoshi (1874–1959), the most influential of Shiki's disciples. In 1912 he formed a small group of women to write and exchange haiku. The group was so successful that four years later he created the "Kitchen Miscellanies" column in *Hototogisu* (The mountain cuckoo), the magazine he edited. It was to include poems on pots and pans, knives, cutting boards, jars, sea breams, cats, dogs, and similar kitchen sights. Also, whenever there was a chance, Kyoshi chose to feature a female poet's haiku on page one of *Hototogisu*. Such early contributors as Hasegawa Kanajo (1887–1969) and Abe Midorijo (1886–1980) became well known, but two latecomers, Takeshita Shizunojo (1887–1951) and Sugita Hisajo (1890–1946), showed greater originality.

Shizunojo and Hisajo, both born in Kyushu, led contrasting lives. Shizunojo was more intellectual and as independent as any man. In her heart she desired to be free from the feudalistic restrictions that still oppressed women, though she did not overtly say so. Well-educated for a woman, she composed poems using Chinese characters and idioms, much as a male poet would. Her haiku are characterized by intellect, verve, and decisiveness, tempered by a maternal tenderness that came to be cherished by a number of young poets. In her later years she helped to found a haiku magazine for university students, many of whom were to lead a number of fields in the following generaton. Hisajo's work, on the other hand, is distinguished by an elegant and sometimes erotic lyricism.

An idealist, she tried to elevate her haiku above earthly reality. Kyoshi described her poetry as "serenely beautiful and highly noble."[8] Hisajo was a devoted disciple of Kyoshi throughout her career, but in 1936, without stating any reasons, Kyoshi suddenly expelled her from membership in the *Hototogisu* circle. She was devastated, as her respect for the magazine was overwhelming. She gradually abandoned haiku and died a disappointed woman.

Despite the progress made by women poets, the haiku world of the first thirty years of the twentieth century was dominated by men, as women in general were preoccupied with cooking, cleaning, and child rearing. Kyoshi and *Hototogisu* were the center of the haiku universe, never deviating from their text that nature should be copied as actually seen. The free-verse haiku movement of Ogiwara Seisensui (1884–1976) and Nakatsuka Ippekirō (1887–1946) in the 1910s largely bypassed female poets. The proletarian movement that swept the entire literary scene in the 1920s had little impact on them. Shizunojo, Hisajo, and other poets of their sex had to struggle hard to establish their identity because they worked in a male world.

The Rise of Women Poets

The situation began to change when some male poets decided to break with tradition. First, Mizuhara Shūōshi (1892–1981) and Yamaguchi Seishi (1901–1994) left *Hototogisu* in 1931 and started their own magazines. Shūōshi distinguished between scientific truth and literary truth, asserting that the latter kind of truth was not just a distinct category but something that enhanced the former. Seishi made haiku look contemporary not only because he used many up-to-date images but because he treated the wasteland of modern life with consummate skill. Hino Sōjō

---

[8] Tomiyasu et al., eds., *Gendai haiku taikei*, 9:53.

(1901–1956), who founded *Kikan* (The flagship) and was expelled from *Hototogisu*, led some young poets close to writing free verse; he tried to deal positively with romantic love and refused to use season words indiscriminately. Nakamura Kusatao (1901–1983), Ishida Hakyō (1913–1969), and Katō Shūson, dissatisfied with realism, founded different magazines and explored human destiny and values. Thus, *Hototogisu* came to see a number of rival magazines. Not long after came the undeclared war with China and the Second World War, which ended in Japan's unconditional surrender; the unprecedented turmoil shook Japanese society from top to bottom. These events allowed a variety of female poets to write more freely than ever before.

Among them was Hashimoto Takako (1899–1963), who first contributed haiku to *Hototogisu* but later left it for another magazine. Talented and beautiful, she married a wealthy businessman and enjoyed a life of affluence, but her husband soon died, leaving her with four girls to bring up. Basic to her poetry was a sense of loneliness, a sense conveyed through various images that reflect different aspects of herself. "When singing of an old woman or a little girl," she said, "I cannot help perceiving her in connection with my life."[9] Trying to describe her subject objectively, she seldom failed to suggest that her solitary existence was extremely lively and emotional.

Mitsuhashi Takajo (1899–1972) was a more daring stylist. As a young girl she wrote *tanka*, then she became a haiku poet when she married and found that haiku was her husband's hobby. At first contributing regularly to a couple of magazines, she soon abandoned them and wrote independently, gradually being attracted to a new movement that at times opposed *Hototogisu*. She found that confinement in one school stifled her. What she wrote was at times so abstract that it did not look like haiku at all. As she grew older, her haiku became preoccupied with images of old

---

[9] Cited in Saitō et al., eds., *Gendai haiku handobukku*, 76.

age and death, not morbidly, but through a richly imagined world of fantasies that absorbed her to the end of her life.

Compared with Takako and Takajo, Ishibashi Hideno (1909–1947) had a brief life; she began writing poetry by experimenting with both *tanka* and haiku at secondary school. She married the haiku critic Yamamoto Kenkichi (1907–1988). Much of her adult life was lived under the harsh circumstances that arose during and after the Second World War and included the fight with tuberculosis that eventually felled her. She was not well known as a haiku poet when she was alive. Her haiku, written in her spare time, is best when it speaks of her life of dire poverty during the war and its aftermath. Her one volume of haiku was posthumously published by her husband; it won the first Bōsha Prize, a leading haiku award given in honor of Kawabata Bōsha (1900–1941), an illustrious poet.

Several other women poets, as their numbers gradually increased, are worth mentioning here. Nakamura Teijo (1900–1968), a student of Kyoshi's, was a technically accomplished composer of "Kitchen Miscellanies." Hoshino Tatsuko (1903–1984), a daughter of Kyoshi's, composed sensitive haiku on the principle of *shasei*. Suzuki Masajo (b. 1906), a restaurant owner, wrote prolifically and with deep feeling of her checkered life in a great number of haiku. Hosomi Ayako (1907–1997), the second recipient of the Bōsha Prize, was a close observer of nature and fastidious in her choice of words to describe it. Katō Chiyoko (1909–1986), wife of Shūson, produced haiku overflowing with lyricism. The war brought much pain to these and other poets, but they wrote about the life around them and made a diary of their fragmentary art.

After the Second World War

The postwar period brought many controversies to haiku circles. Kuwabara Takeo (1904–1988), a specialist in the

French novel, spurned haiku as a second-rate art, saying its conventions forbade individuality of experience. The critic Yamamoto Kenkichi, on the other hand, valued the convivial and humorous elements in haiku, trying to restore it to its original social context. Imoto Nōichi (1913–1998), a scholar in Japanese literature, saw irony at the center of haiku, while young poets like Kaneko Tōta (b. 1919) began discussing its elements of social responsibilty. While the various arguments raged on, women got together in 1954 and started the magazine *Josei haiku* (Women's haiku) exclusively for female haiku poets, as its name implies. Central to the editorial staff was Katō Chiyoko; haiku poets all over Japan joined in.

Despite their unity in founding *Josei haiku*, the female poets' writings were wildly diverse in this and other publications. At one extreme were the *Hototogisu* poets, who, as ever, emulated Kyoshi and represented nature as it appeared before them. At the other were those poets who produced what amounted to free verse in seventeen syllables, with no season words included. Although the women were not as extreme as the men, the differences between the two factions were unmistakable. The progressive faction formed the Association of Haiku Poets in 1961, splitting away from the Association of Modern Haiku, which had been organized in 1946. Women poets on both sides were more noticeable than ever before. The three described below represent only a small portion of them.

Katsura Nobuko (b. 1914) began writing haiku in *Kikan*, a magazine started by Hino Sōjō that explored innovative topics and techniques. Widowed early in life and made homeless by an air raid, she clung to haiku as her only emotional recourse and outlet. Her second book of haiku is especially well known: entitled *Nyoshin* (The female body, 1955), it encompassed her feelings as a woman. Her passion and eroticism have subsided over the years, but her pride in her identity as a woman has not. To quote her own words, "What I have received from my ancient ancestors issues forth in fire when given a chance."[10] In her old age, composing haiku has become as natural to her as speaking.

Yoshino Yoshiko (b. 1915) wrote free verse before taking up haiku. Her poems are often subjective: she makes clear where she stands, suggests how she feels. Lyrical and full of sentiment, her haiku range far in search of timeless values. She has published five collections of haiku so far. In addition, *Budding Sakura* and *Tsuru*, selections of her haiku in English translation, appeared in 2000 and 2001, respectively. A globe-trotter, she has traveled widely and made a number of friends internationally.

Tsuda Kiyoko (b. 1920), first a *tanka* poet, turned to haiku when she met Hashimoto Takako. Yet she is more overtly realistic than her teacher in dealing with her subjects. In this respect she seems to be closer to Yamaguchi Seishi, whom she respected as her ultimate master. "Composing haiku is like cooking," she is quoted as having said. "All I do is cook and offer it to my master. Whether he eats it or not does not matter with me. That is my attitude."[11] Her latest book, *Muhō* (No directions, 2000), was awarded the Dakotsu Prize, which was created in honor of the distinguished haiku poet Iida Dakotsu (1885–1962).

Women's Haiku Today

From the 1960s to the 1980s, Japan changed from a defeated nation to a rising industrial power at which the world marveled. The Tokyo Summer Olympics in 1964, the Osaka World Fair in 1970, the Sapporo Winter Olympics in 1972, the Okinawa Marine Fair in 1975, the Kobe Port Island Fair in 1981, the Tsukuba Science World Fair in 1985, the Seto Bridge opening in 1988 — each event

---

[10] Ibid., 27.
[11] Tomiyasu et al., *Gendai haiku taikei*, 12:147.

heralded a leap forward in the Japanese standard of living. Women, especially, were helped by the availability of conveniences such as prepared foods, washing machines, and motor vehicles, all of which saved them a good deal of time and labor. The new leisure time was spent in a myriad of ways, including attendance at poetry circles. It is not surprising that the number of women who wrote haiku increased markedly during this period, even surpassing that of male poets.

Inahata Teiko (b. 1931), a granddaughter of Kyoshi, became editor of *Hototogisu* in 1979. That haiku imitate nature and its seasonal changes is a basic idea in which she has believed unwaveringly since her youth. Many of her haiku are distilled from observation of her own surroundings. It was in this general spirit that she founded the Japanese Association of Traditional Haiku and took its leadership in 1987. She has traveled to various places, including China, Europe, and the United States, to spread her beliefs. She encourages people to use haiku to effect a return to nature and, through nature, to their forgotten inner selves.

More free and experimental is Uda Kiyoko (b. 1935), a disciple of Katsura Nobuko. Her haiku poems, however, are more difficult to understand than Nobuko's, for they are more abstract and have images that can be interpreted in multiple ways. Part of the reason may be that she communicates with many schools of haiku, including the most avant-garde. Once she went so far as to join Nakagami Kenji (1946–1992) in searching for cultural ancestry in Kumano on the Kii Peninsula.[12] She has also published many essays on the history and criticism of haiku.

Uda's friend Kuroda Momoko (b. 1938) values season words in haiku, so much so that she wants to observe

---

[12] The Kumano region was Nakagami's birthplace and the setting of many of his novels. It was not only a geographical space but a mythic land from which many of his characters emerged.

through her own eyes the objects signified by those words. Thus she often goes on *ginkō*, a tour to write haiku, by herself or with a group of poets. On these she produces many haiku and abandons almost as many. She has done this throughout her career in spite of her busy schedule at a large public relations company, where she worked for a number of years. Vitality is her watchword; she composes haiku with an energy that is irresistible. This volume's title is taken from one of her haiku.

Tsuji Momoko (b. 1945), who also writes free verse, has a talent for making haiku accessible to a wide audience. "At least," she says, "humor is a secret malevolence directed with hurricane force against the injustice of mankind's existence. I want to laugh at the malevolence and explode the energy of living at this moment."[13] Her haiku are characterized by humor that lies beneath the surface. She uses fashionable terms, foreign words, slang—all kinds of words, forging them into a new kind of haiku. Anything in our life can be made into haiku— that is Tsuji Momoko's motto.

Katayama Yumiko (b. 1952) is known as a writer of criticism as well as of haiku. "Sexually, a man and a woman are entirely different," she says. "In a literary genre known as haiku, doesn't a woman have a choice to make use of the sexual difference and explore a world that men cannot enter and sing of?"[14] She went on to comment on one hundred contemporary women' poets, selecting a few haiku from each for explication. Yet a majority of her own haiku do not seem to be particularly feminine. Her sharp senses, perhaps honed by her childhood near the seacoast, are apparent in the imaganative diction of her poetry.

Mayuzumi Madoka (b. 1965) represents an even newer generation of haiku poets. Her haiku are best known for

---

[13] Sōda, ed., *Gendai haiku shūsei*, 340.
[14] Katayama, *Teihon gendai haiku joryū hyakunin*, 9.

romantic love as it is conceived by young men and women today. The love suggested by her is modern, frank, and a touch melancholy. She has also written many haiku that have nothing to do with love affairs. Of the motivation to compose haiku, she says: "The impatience at not being able to say what I most want to say, the misery of not being able to hear what I most want to hear, the pain of not being able to meet when I most want to meet—I decided to sing these out in seventeen syllabes instead of shedding tears."[15] She writes not only of pain and misery but of joy and anger and all other shades of emotion that come to her in daily life. And she does so using the language that is as contemporary as any young woman may use in today's Japan.

What Women Have Contributed to Haiku

"Haiku is neither 'feminine' nor 'masculine,'" says Tsuji Momoko. "All we have are lyrical haiku and comic, humorous haiku."[16] Most poets would agree. As a serious poetic form, haiku is designed to suggest a slice of reality in seventeen Japanese syllables, using as a cue some word that evokes one of the seasons. The reality in question may range from a picturesque scene with a strong emotional impact to an incongruous situation that makes one smile. These two poles attain classic expression in Bashō's *sabi* and *karumi*: an austere beauty arising from the poet's identification with vegetable and mineral nature and a humorous ambience seen from the poet's contemplative point of view.

Haiku shun straight expression of overpowering emotion, which is the realm of *tanka*. It also avoids satirical or

---

[15] Postscript in Mayuzumi, *B-men no natsu*, 225.
[16] *Haiku*, September 1997, 88.

burlesque critique of the human condition, which is the favorite theme of *senryū*. Most often a haiku is a poem where one or more images present the germs of what the poet feels—the fountainhead, in fact, of her inspiration. The value of an individual haiku depends upon the depth in which its images probe human reality. Poets, men and women alike, try to extend this depth as much as possible. Thus most of the haiku written in the past have been poems that aimed at such effects, regardless of the poet's gender.

On the whole, however, it can be said that women excel in what Tsuji Momoko calls "lyrical haiku." Female poets tend to use the conventions of haiku for the carefully wrought expression of spontaneous emotion. Where men tend to step back and observe, women, in general more persistently serious, often do not do so; sportiveness and humor are not leading concerns. The lyrical tradition of *tanka*, which has long captivated them, might be operative here. The following haiku by Takeshita Shizunojo is a good example:

grief and anger—	*hifun ari*
I spit out black, black	*hakishi suika no*
watermelon seeds	*shushi kuroku*

The poet expresses her bitter emotion as she eats a slice of watermelon. It is as though the black color of the seeds has assumed her grief and anger. Or consider this well-known poem by Hashimoto Takako:

a flash of lightning	*inabikari*
coming from the north, I look	*kita yori sureba*
to the north	*kita wo miru*

Here, the poet's emotion is not specified in the typical haiku manner; what matters here is the existential loneliness of the poet's looking to the north. The extraordinary degree of her solitude is suggested by the instantaneous strength of the lightning and the freezing cold of the north. More recently, Mayuzumi Madoka has written:

choosing a swimsuit—	*mizugi erabu*
when did his eyes	*itsu shika kare no*
replace mine?	*me to natte*

The poet, on selecting a swimsuit at a department store, realizes she has unconsciously traded her own tastes for her boyfriend's. Suddenly she recovers herself, and at that instant the haiku emerges.

The last example is especially typical of women's haiku, because the poet has become conscious of the male gaze. Traditionally, of course, women have gained their status by being selected by men for their physique. Beautiful female bodies are objects of men's longing and desire, and women are keenly aware of how beauty passes. Thus the fading beauty of a face is mourned in Enomoto Seifu's haiku:

unchanging dolls' faces—	*hina no kao*
I've had no choice, except	*ware zehi naku mo*
to grow old	*oinikeri*

The poet notices that the dolls, which she used to see at the Girls' Festival when she was little, have the same faces although she is now an old woman. The theme of age and mortality is common to both sexes, yet the focus on facial and bodily beauty is particularly feminine. In modern times, Katsura Nobuko's haiku has a voluptuous woman taking a bath:

snow on the window—	*mado no yuki*
a female body makes hot water	*nyotai nite yu wo*
overflow the tub	*afureshimu*

The nude figure is proudly described in a setting that evokes comfort and self-indulgence. Against the snow on the window, the female body makes an erotic impression. This concern with the body continues to the time of one's death, as seen in a haiku Hashimoto Takako wrote just before her last admission to a hospital:

on a snowy day	*yuki no hi no*
my bathed body, a finger	*yokushin isshi*
a toe—I love all of it	*isshi itoshi*

This is an extreme instance of self-love. The poet loves every part of her body until death takes it away.

This trend toward emphasis on the body in women's haiku has led to a more direct expression of physical relationship between the sexes. Haiku has traditionally refrained from open treatment of love and romance, but in the last half century some female poets have become bolder and less inhibited. The loosening of sexual taboos after the Second World War made it possible for haiku to move fearlessly into this hitherto prohibited area. For instance, a metaphor for the male sexual organ appears prominently in a haiku by Yoshino Yoshiko:

the bamboo plant	*take kawa wo*
shedding its sheath	*nugu onna-ra no*
in front of women	*kakomu naka*

Female genitals are suggested in a love scene presented by Katsura Nobuko:

beyond the dark	*i wo nugishi*
where I've disrobed	*yami no anata ni*
an iris in bloom	*ayame saku*

Bamboo and an iris, both images from nature, have taken on an eroticism that they ordinarily do not carry. Other such images have been used in similar ways by other women poets in recent times.

Female poets who prefer not to deal intimately with love still tend to be more personal and familial than social. Until late, a large majority of women spent most of their time cooking meals, cleaning homes, and bringing up children. Takahama Kyoshi had this in mind when he started the "Kitchen Miscellanies" feature for women in his magazine. So, too, did Katō Shūson when he advised a young woman to get married before starting to learn about haiku. The same theme appears in a premodern poem by Chiyojo:

morning glories—	asagao ya
the person who wakes others	okoshita mono wa
doesn't get to see the flowers	hana mo mizu

The mistress who gets up earlier than the others to prepare breakfast has no time to see the morning glories in bloom. Compare a haiku by Ishibashi Hideno:

chapped hands	akagari ya
and no rice—as I weep	ii hori nakeba
a monkey's face	saru no kao

This was written after the Second World War, when there was severe shortage of rice and indeed of anything else to eat. As a housewife the poet has to laugh off the situation, but her laughter ends up in "a monkey's face"—half grinning and half weeping. While there are men's haiku implicitly protesting war or government policy, a large majority of women's haiku remain in the personal or domestic domain.

There can be no doubt, however, that the features of haiku cultivated by female poets will be extended further in the future. Lyrical haiku, physical haiku, erotic haiku, domestic haiku—they will continue to be composed by women. At the same time, women will be producing more of the kind of haiku that have hitherto been the special province of male poets. Humorous and comic haiku, for instance, though traditionally written by men, are seen more conspicuously in the works of women poets like Tsuji Momoko and Mayuzumi Madoka.

one who loves someone	*koi seshi hito*
with the one who doesn't	*koi naki hito to*
drinks beer	*biiru kumu*

This haiku by Tsuji Momoko presents two young people who currently have little in common. We feel as if we were eavesdropping on their conversation.

Today, of the estimated ten million people who write haiku, women far outnumber men. There are well over one hundred and fifty haiku magazines headed by female poets, and they do not lack for female subscribers. *Josei haiku*, a haiku magazine exclusively for women, ceased publication in 1999 because the very term "women's haiku" had effectively lost its meaning. Is it safe to say, then, that women today have reached equality with men in writing haiku? Certainly women are no longer seen as fifth-class poets, nor are they treated only as vessels for bearing an heir. Haiku as a male-oriented genre has disappeared. Yet it is too early to say that the traditional patriarchal attitude has vanished, that the sexual bias against women is gone. We will have to wait until well into the twenty-first century—or later.

Far
Beyond
the Field

Den Sutejo
1633–1698

Den Sutejo lived in the same period as Bashō and belonged to the same school of *haikai*, the Teimon; she also shared the same mentor in her youth, Kitamura Kigin (1624–1705). It is tempting to speculate that the two poets had a chance to meet in Kyoto, where Kigin resided. But such a meeting is unlikely to have taken place, since Sutejo was a married woman whose family considerably outranked Bashō's in social status.

Sutejo was born in 1633, the eldest daughter of an old, illustrious samurai family that lived in a small town in the mountainous area northwest of Kyoto. Her parents, brothers, and many of her other relatives were fond of learning, and she too received the highest level of humanistic education available at the time. Writing haiku and *renku* was part of that education, and her talent for them blossomed after she married her stepmother's son, Suenari, who wrote poetry for a hobby. The 1650s and 1660s were the peak period of her *haikai* activities. Her responsibilities as the mother of six children and mistress of a large samurai household gradually exhausted her creative energy. After Suenari's death in 1674, she began to vent her grief and loneliness in *tanka*, a more lyrical verse form. In 1681 she became a Buddhist nun and moved to Kyoto. Her family belonged to the Pure Land sect of Buddhism, which was popular at the time. She was in search of spiritual enlightenment, but the sect's teachings do not seem to have given her the kind of help she wanted. In 1686 she was converted to the Zen sect and began studying under the noted monk Bankei (1622–1693). She moved to Himeji, where his temple was located, and spent the rest of her life there as a Zen devotee. By the time of her death on 4 September 1698, a number of nuns had gathered around her residence seeking her guidance in Zen. They hardly knew Sutejo had once been a haiku poet.

the moon looks cozier
in the sky when you see it
through the bamboo blind[1]

getting used
to hardship—a bride-grass
in the snow[2]

DEN SUTEJO 3

---

[1] In the *haikai* tradition, the image of the moon indicates autumn. The bamboo blind, which has been hanging to keep out the sun all summer, looks a little dusty—and adds a cozier feeling to the scene—in early autumn.

[2] A play on the word "bride-grass" (*yomena*), which is a species of wild chrysanthemum. In premodern Japan, a married woman usually lived with her husband's parents, whom she was expected to serve with the utmost loyalty and reverence. Here, the new bride is starting to experience the chill of these obligations as the marriage, like winter, sets in.

tsuki ya sora ni iyoge ni miyuru sudare goshi (Ogata et al., vol. 7)

uki naka ni narete yukima no yomena kana (Furuya, vol. 4)

let us start picking—
don't drop herbs from your basket
or anything else[1]

the princess pine
clad in thin snow—
you're a light dresser![2]

DEN SUTEJO

[1] The haiku alludes to the first poem of the eighth-century anthology *Man'yōshū* (The collection of ten thousand leaves), which begins:

With a basket, a pretty basket,
with a trowel, a pretty trowel,
a maiden picking herbs on this hill—
I want to ask about your home,
won't you tell me your name?

Sutejo's haiku seems to parody this poem of courtship, for in it she advises the maiden, as one woman to another, not to let anything drop, that is to say, not to give her name easily when approached by a man. The original Japanese poem makes clever use of the word *wakana*, which means both "young herb" and "my name."

[2] A princess pine (*himematsu*) is another name for a red pine.

iza tsumamu wakana morasu na kago no uchi (Ogata et al., vol. 7)

himematsu no katabira yuki ya date usugi (Hisamatsu and Imoto, vol. 2)

the branch of plum blossoms—
strong fragrance
of the lord I love[1]

making sure we know
that autumn is here, a leaf
from the empress tree[2]

DEN SUTEJO 5

---

[1] The haiku is probably based on an anonymous *tanka* that appears in *Kokin waka shū* (The collection of ancient and modern poems, 905):

the strong fragrance	*satsuki matsu*
of mandarin orange blossoms	*hana tachibana no*
awaiting the fifth month	*ka wo kageba*
reminds me of the scented	*mukashi no hito no*
sleeves of someone I used to love	*sode no ka zo suru*

[2] The poem alludes to a maxim: "The fall of a single leaf suggests the coming of autumn to the entire world." The empress tree (*Paulownia tomentosa*) is deciduous and has very large leaves.

ume ga e wa omou kisama no kaori kana (Furuya, vol. 4)

kuru aki no kirigiwa misuru hitoha kana (Hisamatsu and Imoto, vol. 2)

day-darkener cicada,
know you not the day darkens
without your help?[1]

pine mushrooms
live a thousand years
in one autumn[2]

DEN SUTEJO

---

[1] A day darkener (*higurashi*) is a species of cicada with a sweet, high-pitched cry. It is so called because it sings late in the day.
[2] A pine mushroom (*matsutake*) is so named because it sprouts under pine trees. In Japan, pine trees were once believed to live for a thousand years. Buddhism emphasizes that each living thing possesses a different sense of time.

higurashi ya sutete oite mo kururu hi wo (Furuya, vol. 4)

matsutake wa tada hitoaki wo chitose kana (Hisamatsu and Imoto, vol. 2)

is that a cloud
or a standing screen? again
the moon is hiding her face[1]

too impatient to wait
for summer, plum blossoms
in a white suit of snow[2]

DEN SUTEJO

[1] The poem describes a scene of moon viewing, which was a traditional social activity in mid-autumn. The moon is likened to a shy young lady reluctant to come out from behind a screen.
[2] Plum blossoms, covered with thin snow, have donned a *shiragasane*, a white garment customarily worn on the first day of summer.

kumo ya kichō hata kakuretaru tsuki no kao (Hisamatsu and Imoto, vol. 2)

natsu matade baika no yuki ya shiragasane (Ibid.)

adorned with raindrops
from the shower, a sparkling
princess azalea[1]

by the millet ears
how insignificant they look!
lady flower seeds[2]

DEN SUTEJO

---

[1] The haiku sketches a wild azalea in bloom that looks more beautiful after the rain. The poet's clever use of the word "princess" (*hime*) brings together the images of the Shining Princess (a legendary princess) and the "princess" variety of azalea.

[2] *Ominaeshi* (*Patrinia scabiosifolia*), literally "lady flower," is also called *awabana* or "millet flower" because its flowers' color is similar to cooked millet. A single ear of millet produces a proverbially large number of grains. This haiku may have a metaphorical meaning, a lady flower standing for the poet's work.

nureiro ya ame no shita teru himetsutsuji (Hisamatsu and Imoto, vol. 2)

awa no ho ya mi wa kazu naranu ominaeshi (Ogata et al., vol. 7)

would that the cuckoo of old
would let fall its cry, even as
this old rain keeps falling![1]

New Year's soup —
I make a thousand shavings
of dried bonito[2]

DEN SUTEJO

[1] Since ancient times, the mountain cuckoo's cry, rarely heard in urban areas, has been a treasured exprience for poets. The humor of this haiku revolves around the word *furu*, which means at once "old" and "to fall."
[2] As a housewife, the poet dutifully prepares soup on New Year's morning, with her heartfelt greetings as the main ingredient. Shavings of dried bonito are used for seasoning. The usual New Year's prayer in Japan is for "one thousand" — that is, a great many — returns of the auspicious day to oneself and one's family.

nakase ta ya samidare no furu hototogisu (Hisamatsu and Imoto, vol. 2)

zōni ni ya chiyo no kazu kaku hanagatsuo (Furuya, vol. 4)

last night's bloom
lasting into this morning—
snow on the trees[1]

is there
a shortcut through the clouds,
summer moon?[2]

DEN SUTEJO

---

[1] The humor of this haiku lies in the clever play on the Japanese word *saku*, which functions both as an adjective meaning "last" and as a verb meaning "to bloom."
[2] The haiku alludes to many classical *tanka* that sang of the brevity of a summer night, such as this one included in *Kokin waka shū*:

the summer night wanes	natsu no yo wa
while the hours of the evening	mada yoi nagara
have hardly passed—	akenuru wo
whereabouts in the clouds	kumo no izuko ni
has the moon taken her lodgings?	tsuki yadoruran

kesa mireba hana zo sakuya no kigi no yuki (Hisamatsu and Imoto, vol. 2)

kumoji ni mo chikamichi aru ya natsu no tsuki (Zoku haiku kōza, vol. 1)

do you paint your eyebrows
using water for a mirror,
riverside willow?[1]

gale in the mountains—
watch how the fallen blossoms
carpet the water[2]

DEN SUTEJO 11

[1] The willow tree, because it is pliant and graceful, has been compared to a young woman in Japan since ancient times.
[2] The humor of this haiku turns on the Japanese word *ika* (how), which happens to be part of another word, *ikada* (raft). *Hana ikada* (blossom raft) describes how the petals gather on the water.

mizukagami mite ya mayu kaku kawayanagi (Kuriyama et al.)

yama no arashi ika bakari zo ya hana ikada (*Zoku haiku kōza*, vol. 1)

do you bloom
just to teach the world,
cherry blossoms?[1]

                              not a single leaf—
                              even the moon does not lodge
                              in this willow tree

[1] Cherry blossoms teach the evanescence of life on earth.

hana wa yo no tameshi ni saku ya hitosakari (Furuya, vol. 4)

kare hatete tsuki mo yadoranu yanagi kana (Ibid.)

Kawai Chigetsu
1634?–1718

If Bashō, a lifelong bachelor, knew one woman with whom he could joke and relax, that woman was Kawai Chigetsu. They were not only teacher and student in *haikai* but very close friends outside that relationship. Their closeness is suggested, for instance, by a little incident that took place one day in 1690, when Chigetsu begged for a keepsake from her teacher, who was soon to conclude his stay at her house. Bashō reportedly replied, "Someone who is nearing her sixtieth year asks me for a keepsake. How very depressing! She must want me to die before her!" Laughing, he obliged: he gave his older friend a portrait of himself and a copy of his *haibun*, *Genjūan no ki* (The record of the Genjū Hut).[1]

Little is known about Chigetsu's early years. It is believed that she was born at Usa, near Kyoto, and served at the imperial court when she was young. Bashō was some ten years her junior. Later, she married Kawai Saemon, a merchant who operated a large carting business in Ōtsu, a city on the southwest shore of Lake Biwa. Because they had no children when her husband died in or around 1686, she adopted her younger brother Otokuni (1657–1720) as the heir to the family business. Apparently, she became serious about writing haiku under the influence of Otokuni, who had been a student of Bashō's. She and Otokuni often invited the great poet to their house and composed haiku and

---

[1] Kawai Otokuni, *Bashō-ō gyōjōki*. Cited in Kawashima, *Joryū haijin*, 38.

renku with him. It was Chigetsu and Otokuni's wife who made the garment for Bashō to wear on his journey to the world beyond. She seems to have been an outgoing, vivacious, rather carefree person. Once, when Otokuni was on a trip, he thought fondly of his home and wondered what his elder sister might be doing in her kitchen:

spring nightfall—	*haru no yo no*
Chigetsu must be burning	*mochi ya Chigetsu no*
her rice cakes till black	*kogasuran*[2]

Unlike Sutejo, who entered the convent, or Sonome who became a professional *haikai* teacher in later life, Chigetsu remained at home. She continued to enjoy family life even after shaving her head upon her husband's death. She died a contented grandmother in 1718.

---

[2] Cited in Kawashima, *Joryū haijin*, 35.

alone in bed
I hear a male mosquito
humming a sad tune[1]

under the harvest moon
awestruck crows
curb their voices

KAWAI CHIGETSU

[1] Written in or around 1686, shortly after her husband died.

hitorine ya yo wataru oka no koe wabishi (Ogata et al., vol. 7)

meigetsu ni karasu wa koe wo nomarekeri (Ibid.)

pointing their fingers
and standing on tiptoe
children admire the moon

flowers of rice —
let them be my offering
to the Buddha[1]

---

[1] Chigetsu wrote this when she paid a visit to her teacher Bashō one day in 1690. At the time, Bashō was staying in a small cottage called the Genjū Hut, which held a Buddhist altar. Flowers of rice are small and inconspicuous, yet the poet thought they possessed the kind of unobtrusive beauty Bashō favored.

yubi sashite nobi suru chigo no tsukimi kana (Sekimori)

ine no hana kore wo hotoke no miyage kana (Horikiri, vol. 2)

spring snow
revives the greenery
then goes

mountain azaleas
calling out to the ocean
in the setting sun

KAWAI CHIGETSU

shirayuki no wakaba koyashite kienikeri (Horikiri, vol. 2.)

yamatsutsuji umi ni miyo to ya yūhikage (Ogata et al., vol. 7)

a bamboo bud
breaking out of its layered sheath—
a warrior in arms!

like scarecrows
as solitary and charming—
my sister nuns[1]

---

[1] This poem was written in or around 1692, on the seventh anniversary of her husband's death, an important event in Buddhist thought. By this time, many of her friends were also widows and had become lay nuns like herself.

takenoko ya kawa tsuki kowashi kabuto musha (Ogata et al., vol. 7)

kagashi ni mo awaresa makeji ama nakama (Ibid.)

the mountain cherry tree
shedding its blossoms—in the brook
a waterwheel

they wait for spring—
stuck under the ice
trash and rubbish

yamazakura chiru ya ogawa no mizuguruma (Ogata et al., vol. 7)

matsu haru ya kōri ni majiru chiri akuta (Ibid.)

a bush warbler—
my hands in the kitchen sink
rest for a while

flowing here and there
in the street toward the year's end
sooty water[1]

[1] Written on the thirtieth day of the twelfth lunar month, traditionally the annual Housecleaning Day.

uguisu ni temoto yasumemu nagashimoto (Ogata et al., vol. 7)

nagaruru ya shiwasu no machi no susu no shiru (Horikiri, vol. 2)

the reservoir—
tadpoles appear hatching
in warmer water

bindweed flowers—
each face saying
it did not rain enough[1]

---

[1] The Japanese word for bindweed is *hirugao*, literally "daytime face." Its flowers are shaped like those of morning glory (*asagao*, "morning face"), though they bloom in the daytime.

tameike ni kawazu umaruru nurumi kana (Hisamatsu and Imoto, vol. 5)

hirugao ya ame furi taranu hana no kao (Ibid.)

a wintry gust
with no color to show
with no leaves to rip

                                grandchildren come
                                and drag me out of bed—
                                the year's end

KAWAI CHIGETSU

kogarashi ya iro ni mo miezu chiri mo sezu (Ogata et al., vol. 7)

magodomo ni hiki okosarete toshi no kure (Horikiri, vol. 2)

one with a flower
the other without—
two poppies in a vase

faintly, faintly
a smell of charcoal—
the footwarmer on a spring day[1]

---

[1] A footwarmer is a small stove with live charcoal in it. People covered it with a quilt and warmed their feet around it.

aru to naki to nihon sashikeri keshi no hana (Ogata et al., vol. 7)

honobono to sumi mo niou ya harugotatsu (Horikiri, vol. 2)

crying as though
the sole owner of all loneliness
a dove in autumn[1]

the earthenware mortar—
its sound portends snow
near the year's end

---

[1] This poem probably alludes to a *tanka* in *Shin kokin waka shū* (The new collection of ancient and modern poems) by the priest Saigyō (1118–1190):

on a tree standing	*furuhata no*
by the cliff in an old farm	*soba no tatsu ki ni*
a dove—	*iru hato no*
how lonely his voice	*tomo yobu koe no*
calling for a friend this evening	*sugoki yūgure*

sabishisa wo wagamonogao ya aki no hato (Furuya, vol. 4)

suribachi no oto ya shiwasu no yukige kana (Horikiri, vol. 2)

Shiba Sonome
1664–1726

Shiba Sonome is at once famous and notorious in the history of haiku. She is famous because, as mentioned in the Introduction, Bashō visited her home in 1694 and wrote a haiku comparing her to a pure white chrysanthemum. But she gained notoriety when Bashō died two weeks later, giving rise to a rumor that the cause of his last ailment was the mushrooms she had served him at her house. The rumor had no solid basis, for Bashō had been in frail health for quite some time. Nevertheless, the innuendoes seemed to alienate her from Bashō while he yet lived and from his leading disciples. As far as the surviving records indicate, she never visited him on his deathbed, and after he died she seldom worked with the poets of the mainstream Bashō school.

Sonome was born in 1664 near the Grand Shinto Shrines in Ise Province (Mie Prefecture). She must have been exposed to haiku early in life, because writing *haikai* had been popular among the residents of Ise since the early sixteenth century. And her interest in it must have intensified when she married Shiba Ichiyū (d. 1703?), an eye doctor who wrote haiku and *renku* for a hobby. When Bashō visited Ise in the spring of 1688, Ichiyū and Sonome welcomed him to their home. In 1692 they moved to Osaka, and Sonome began to help the family finances as a professional judge in public *haikai* contests. It seems that she aggressively sought to befriend prestigious poets in her new city. She not only invited Bashō to her home but actively made contact with noted poets outside of

Bashō's school, such as Ihara Saikaku. Ichiyū's death, however, seems to have led her to restart life in an entirely new environment. In 1704 she moved to Edo and, while succeeding her husband as an eye doctor, continued her work as a *haikai* teacher and judge. It was there that she compiled the anthology *Kiku no chiri* (Chrysanthemum rubbish), collecting 687 verses by 378 poets both living and dead. Her poetic activities did not wane after she became a lay nun in 1718. When she reached her sixtieth year in 1723, she commemorated the occasion by completing another *haikai* anthology entitled *Tsuru no tsue* (The crane's staff), which comprised contributions from ninety-nine poets. She died on 21 May 1726.

it stands out
even before blooming—
a wild violet

At Taima Temple[1]

first summer clothes—
a woman who does not weave
feels a deep guilt

---

[1] At Taima Temple in Yamato Province (Nara Prefecture) there was a mandala said to be woven by a legendary princess.

sakanu ma mo mono ni magirenu sumire kana (Jambor)

koromogae mizukara oranu tsumi fukashi (Ibid.)

dirt crumbling
from the low hillside —
a bamboo bud

the insects' chirp
as night deepens
sinks into the stones

SHIBA SONOME

takenoko ni kozaka no tsuchi no kuzurekeri (Jambor)

mushi no ne ya yo fukete shizumu ishi no naka (Ibid.)

in my paper kerchief
a wild violet
has long since wilted

on my back a baby
playing with my hair—
it's really hot!

hanagami no ai ni shioruru sumire kana (Jambor)

outa ko ni kami naburaruru atsusa kana (Ibid.)

daikon turnips
hardening underground—
a traveler feels the cold

putting a handkerchief
atop my hat to dry—
it's really hot!

daikon ni mi no iru tabi no samusa kana (Jambor)

tenogoi mo kasa de kawakasu atsusa kana (Ibid.)

hitting the tree leaves
and breaking them to pieces—
the cold

most of them
don't resemble their name—
lady flowers[1]

---

[1] A lady flower has small pink flowers on its straggling branches, creating a rather untidy impression.

kigi no ha ni sakete kudakete samusa kana (Jambor)

ōkata wa na ni ninu mono wo ominaeshi (Ibid.)

some for admiring blossoms in
others for being admired—
the ladies' hats

how cool it feels
to place my forehead
on the tatami floor!

SHIBA SONOME

hana miru mo ari mirareru mo ari kasa sugata (Jambor)

suzushisa ya hitai wo atete aodatami (Ibid.)

when you grow old
even mice avoid you—
how cold it is!

longing for someone
I sit by the gate and draw
eyebrows on a melon

SHIBA SONOME

toshi yoreba nezumi mo hikanu samusa kana (Jambor)

hito min to uri ni mayu kaku hashii kana (Ibid.)

some blossoms there are
that nobody sees —
an oak deep in the woods[1]

the harvest moon —
near the bridges of a *koto*
chestnut husks[2]

---

[1] Probably inspired by Bashō's haiku:

few in this world	*yo no hito no*
notice those blossoms —	*mitsukenu hana ya*
a chestnut by the eaves	*noki no kuri*

[2] This is a scene after a moon-viewing party where someone played a *koto*, a musical instrument consisting of many strings stretched over a convex sounding board. Chestnuts were served as refreshments.

yo ni hito no shiranu hana ari miyama shii (Jambor)

meigetsu ya kotoji ni sawaru kuri no kawa (Ibid.)

farewell to autumn—
stars sparkle on the water
of the twentieth night[1]

dogs howling
at the sound of leaves—
storm on the way!

SHIBA SONOME

[1] The poem refers to the twentieth night of the ninth lunar month, which falls in October or early November. The moon does not rise as early as on the fifteenth night.

yuku aki ya hatsuka no mizu ni hoshi no teri (Kuriyama et al.)

ha no oto ni inu hoekakaru arashi kana (Jambor)

Love

chilly night—
in the ghastly lamplight
razor-sharp eyebrows[1]

                                    bald mountains
                                    offering nothing
                                    autumn can get grip on

[1] The scene depicts a woman waiting a long time for a lover's visit.

sayuru yo no tomoshibi sugoshi mayu no ken (Jambor)

hageyama wa aki no toritsuku iro mo nashi (Ibid.)

Chiyojo
1703–1775

Critical opinion of Chiyojo's poetry has ranged from one extreme to another. In premodern Japan, her literary fame almost equalled Bashō's. During her lifetime, her verses appeared in more than one hundred books of *haikai*; few anthologists of the time would have dared to exclude her work. So high was her reputation nationally that the lord of Kaga (Ishikawa Prefecture), her province, commissioned her in 1763 to make fifteen fans and six hanging scrolls with her poems written on them; they were to be included among the shogun's gifts to envoys from Korea. In the twentieth century, however, Chiyojo's haiku came under scathing attack from both scholars and practicing poets. Takahama Kyoshi, the most influential haiku poet of the century, repeatedly condemned her poetry as conceited and phony. No less unflattering was the opinion of the eminent haiku scholar Ebara Taizō (1894–1948), who found her work emotionally shallow and declared: "It goes without saying that she should be considered less than a third-rate poet."[1] Today there is a trend in favor of reevaluating her work by paying more attention to the poems that were less popular in premodern times.

Despite her fame while alive, many blanks remain in Chiyojo's biography. There is no conclusive evidence to show whether she had a family name or how she began to write haiku or even if she ever married. At least it is certain

[1] Ebara, *Haiku hyōshaku*, 2:95.

that she was born in 1703 near Kanazawa, on the coast of the Sea of Japan, and that her father made a living by mounting pictures on scrolls and screens, a profession to which she was to succeed after his death. When she was sixteen, Kagami Shikō, a haiku master who popularized a plain style, visited her house and wrote *renku* with her and other local poets. Immediately he recognized her talent, and his lavish praise launched her on a productive career as a poet. In later years she made trips to various parts of Japan to exchange haiku or write *renku* with other poets of Shikō's school. She traveled to Kyoto at least three times, once extending the journey to Edo and other eastern towns and not returning home for two years. Some of the poets she met during her travels, such as Nakagawa Otsuyū (1675–1739), were prominent figures in contemporary haiku circles, and her acquaintance with them helped to spread her name even wider. In 1754 she became a nun, calling herself Chiyoni or Soen, but she did not stop writing verses. *Chiyoni kushū* (The collected haiku of Chiyoni), containing 546 of her haiku, was published in 1764. Seven years later it was followed by another collection, *Matsu no koe* (The voice of the pine), which included 327 haiku. She died on 2 October 1775, leaving behind more haiku than any other woman poet of premodern Japan.

my well bucket
taken by the morning glory—
this borrowed water

the butterfly
behind, before, behind
a woman on the road

CHIYOJO 39

asagao ni tsurube torarete morai mizu (Nakamoto)

chōchō ya onago no michi no ato ya saki (Ibid.)

morning glories—
the person who wakes others
doesn't get to see the flowers[1]

moonflowers in bloom
when a woman's skin
gleams through the dusk[2]

---

[1] A Japanese housewife always gets up earlier than the rest of the family and busies herself preparing breakfast.
[2] Moonflowers bloom on summer evenings. Many townspeople in premodern Japan, since their houses lacked bathrooms, would take a cold bath in a tub placed outdoors after nightfall.

asagao ya okoshita mono wa hana mo mizu (Nakamoto)

yūgao ya onago no hada no miyuru toki (Ibid.)

it's made me forget
about the rouge on my lips—
a crystalline stream

a white chrysanthemum—
how strange to see it
bloom in the sun

beni saita kuchi mo wasururu shimizu kana (Nakamoto)

shiragiku ya hi ni sakō to wa omowarezu (Ibid.)

something like the voice
of deepening autumn
from a gourd[1]

the first winter shower—
a gust passes
without getting wet

---

[1] This is an empty gourd, across which the autumn wind is blowing. Before glass bottles were imported, the Japanese stored liquids in gourds. They bored a hole through which the seeds were extracted at the top of the gourd, which was then dried until it became hard.

yuku aki no koe mo izuru ya fukube kara (Nakamoto)

hatsushigure kaze mo nurezu ni tōrikeri (Ibid.)

do they flower
dreaming of a spring night?
blossoms out of season

turned into blossoms
or drops of dew?
this morning's snow

haru no yo no yume mite saku ya kaeribana (Nakamoto)

hana to nari shizuku to naru ya kesa no yuki (Ibid.)

spring rain—
all things on earth
becoming beautiful

                              not yet suntanned
                              a village child's complexion—
                              peach blossoms in bloom

harusame ya utsukushū naru mono bakari (Nakamoto)

sato no ko no hada mada shiroshi momo no hana (Ibid.)

a door left open
yet nobody is home—
peach blossoms in bloom

waterweed
floating away, despite
the butterfly's weight on it

to no akete aredo rusu nari momo no hana (Nakamoto)

ukigusa ya chō no chikara no osaete mo (Ibid.)

a dandelion
now and then interrupting
the butterfly's dream

moonlit night—
out on the stone
a cricket singing

tanpopo ya oriori samasu chō no yume (Nakamoto)

tsuki no yo ya ishi ni dete naku kirigirisu (Ibid.)

does it sense
anything that steals by?
snow on the bamboos

loneliness
lies within the listener—
a cuckoo's call

sotto kuru mono ni kizuku ya take no yuki (Nakamoto)

sabishisa wa kiku hito ni koso kankodori (Ibid.)

the harvest moon—
there too is a bird
that seeks the dark[1]

trout going downstream—
day by day the water
frightens me more[2]

---

[1] The poem implies that everyone's taste is different.
[2] Japanese trout (*ayu*), after laying eggs in a river toward the end of autumn, swim downstream to die in the sea.

meigetsu ya yami wo tazunuru tori mo ari (Nakamoto)

ochiayu ya hi ni hi ni mizu no osoroshiki (Ibid.)

Enomoto Seifu
1732–1815

Whereas Chiyojo's reputation has plummeted, Enomoto Seifu's haiku have been accorded ever higher critical acclaim in the twentieth century. The reappraisal of her work started indirectly with Shiki, who gave profuse praise to Buson's poetry for its objective, colorful, and dramatic qualities, the same qualities that characterize Seifu's. Although Shiki himself made no reference to her, his followers were motivated to pay attention to Buson's contemporaries and eventually discovered, or rediscovered, her haiku. Especially since the poet Nishitani Seinosuke (1897–1932) praised her in 1929, her stature as a poet has steadily grown. In 1953 Yamamoto Kenkichi went so far as to say that among premodern women poets who wrote haiku, Seifu was the only one who had left truly outstanding work.

Seifu was born in 1732, the only child of Enomoto Chūzaemon, who headed an old samurai family living in a town some twenty-five miles east of Edo. Her later writings suggest she received a good education, especially in Japanese classics, during her girlhood. Quite likely her interest in haiku started at an early age. It became more serious when her widowed father married a lady who wrote haiku under the *haigō*, or haiku name, of Senchō. She joined a haiku group headed by Shirai Chōsui (1701–1769), a haiku master in Edo, because her stepmother had been his student. Her haiku began to appear in various *haikai* anthologies starting around 1755. She had married by that time and given birth to a son, although, as the only child of the family, she kept the Enomoto name and continued to live in her father's house with her husband, following the general custom. Her poetic output seems to have increased after she became a widow in 1770. By that time her teacher Chōsui had died, and she began working under the guidance of Kaya Shirao (1738–1791), even though she was older than he. Shirao was a more gifted poet than her late teacher, and his advice seems to have helped her. The new teacher and student worked so closely with each other that some have suspected a romantic relationship between the two. When Shirao passed away, Seifu became a nun. Her son, perhaps wanting to help console his grief-stricken mother, compiled *Seifuni kushū* (The collected *haikai* verses of the nun Seifu) two years later. Apparently, she practiced Zen meditation at a temple in Kamakura some time in her last years. She died on 6 February 1815.

at daybreak
speaking to the blossoms
a woman all alone

stillness—
out of the rain a butterfly
roams into my bedroom

akatsuki no hana ni mono iu hitori kana (Nishitani)

shizukanaru ya fushido ni irishi ame no chō (Yamamoto, vol. 4)

rumbles from the rocks—
cherry blossoms in the moonlight
far from the world of men

Enjoying myself at a sake
shop in Kanagawa[1]

like a fish
in the sea, this body of mine
cool in the moonlight

[1] Kanagawa is the modern city of Yokohama. The shop probably overlooked the sea.

iwa no oto tsuki no yozakura hito tōshi (Nishitani)

umi ni sumu uo no goto mi wo tsuki suzushi (Kuriyama et al.)

no more water—
decaying in the ivy
a bamboo drain

that worm-eaten fan
looks charming too—
first summer clothes

mizu taete tsuta ni kuchitaru kakei kana (Nishitani)

mushi hamishi ōgi mo okashi koromogae (Ibid.)

leaves of a palm
staying just as they have been—
autumn comes to a close

a market day in the hills—
hailstones ricochet
off the horns of a cow

ENOMOTO SEIFU

shuro no ha no tada sono mama ni aki kurenu (Yamamoto, vol. 4)

yamaichi ya arare tabashiru ushi no tsuno (Ueno, *Josei haiku no sekai*)

someone's ragball
in the hedge, plum blossoms
fluttering down

shaking sand off
his bristly hair, a sumo wrestler
who's lost the match[1]

---

[1] Professional sumo wrestling was attended only by men. Women, however, could enjoy amateur wrestlers' sumo at various festivals.

yoso no mari kaki ni horori to ume no chiru (Nishitani)

suna furū kamisuji futoshi makezumō (Ueno, *Josei haiku no sekai*)

clustered bush clover—
the wheels of a carriage
squeak in the moonlight

spring departs—
clothes hanging out to dry
at a mountain villa

murahagi ni kuruma no kishiru tsukiyo kana (Nishitani)

yuku ya haru koromo hoshitaru yamayashiki (Ibid.)

clap of a pheasant's wings
as a string on my *koto*
snaps—and night falls

blissfully lying
under the falling blossoms
a skeleton[1]

ENOMOTO SEIFU

[1] There was a widespread famine in Japan between 1782 and 1787. The haiku alludes to a *tanka* in *Sankashū* (The mountain home collection) by the priest Saigyō:

I pray to die	*negawakuba*
under cherry blossoms	*hana no moto ni te*
in spring	*haru shinamu*
when the moon is full	*sono kisaragi no*
in the lunar second month	*mochizuki no koro*

Saigyō's prayer was answered, as he died on the sixteenth of the second lunar month in 1190.

kiji utte koto no o kireshi yūbe kana (Kuriyama et al.)

chiru hana no moto ni medetaki dokuro kana (Ueno, *Josei haiku no sekai*)

an aged butterfly
letting its soul play
with a chrysanthemum

                              departing spring—
                              in a cluster of mugwort
                              human bones

chō oite tamashii kiku ni asobu kana (Ueno, *Josei haiku no sekai*)

yuku haru ya yomogi ga naka no hito no hone (Ibid.)

a bird far away
flying into the clouds
its belly white

Among the least interesting things to look at is an old woman. On an evening that somehow makes me ponder the past and the future, I mutter to myself:

flowers of sorrow in bloom—
walking past my gate
a mirror polisher[1]

---

[1] *U no hana*, literally "flowers of sorrow," refers to deutzia flowers, which bloom in pure white during the summer months. The mirror polisher in the haiku seems to know that the poet is an old woman who has little need for a mirror.

tori tōshi kumo ni iru sa no hara shiroki (Kawashima)

u no hana ya kado wo sugi yuku kagamitogi (Ueno, *Josei haiku no sekai*)

unchanging dolls' faces—
I've had no choice, except
to grow old

Meeting with the priest
Bansetsu at Kenchō Temple[1]

a pheasant's cry—
resounding in the mountain
the voice of silence

ENOMOTO SEIFU

---

[1] Kenchō Temple is a renowned Zen temple in Kamakura.

hina no kao ware zehi naku mo oinikeri (Nishitani)

kigisu naku yama wa musei no hibiki kana (Ueno, *Josei haiku no sekai*)

Tagami Kikusha
1753–1826

Tagami Kikusha once wrote, "My guiding principle has always been to enjoy life."[1] The better to observe this principle, she mastered the arts of painting, calligraphy, *koto* music, *tanka*, Chinese poetry, and, of course, haiku. With the same principle in mind she spent most of her adult life traveling all over Japan, visiting distant places, and meeting all kinds of people. Considering the feudal restrictions placed on women's conduct in those days, Kikusha was a carefree spirit who lived life on her own terms. She was able to do so, however, only after she renounced her femininity at the young age of twenty-seven. One of the associations of her adopted name, Kikusha, is "discarded chrysanthemum."

Kikusha was born Tagami Michi on 8 November 1753, in a village located near the western end of Honshu. Her father was a samurai who also practiced medicine. At the age of sixteen she married a son of an affluent farming family in the same village, but when he died eight years later she returned to her parents' home. By the age of twenty-five, she must have decided to pursue the art of poetry rather than a second marriage, for she adopted the *haigō* Kikusha. In 1780 she had her head shaved at a Buddhist temple, and shortly afterwards she set out on a long journey to northeastern Japan, tracing Bashō's famous itinerary in reverse order. Because she started at the western tip of Honshu, her entire journey was more than twice as long as

---

[1] Hisamatsu and Imoto, eds., *Koten haibungaku taikei*, 16:189.

Bashō's, taking her some two years to complete. Apparently she enjoyed life on the road, for she spent most of the next thirty years traveling. Surviving records show she took two extended trips to Edo, four to Kyushu, and five to Kyoto. Helpful to her on those trips was a nationwide network of poets who belonged to Shikō's school of haiku, of which she was a member. It seems that those poets welcomed her to their homes wherever she went because she appears to have been an affable, charming person with many artistic skills to display. Her skill in painting served her especially well on the road, even enabling her to earn cash here and there. In later years, the lord of her home province became her admirer, and in 1803 he invited her to compose haiku and Chinese verse for him. Her collected verse, *Taorigiku* (Plucked chrysanthemums), was published in 1812 to celebrate her sixtieth birthday by Japanese count. She died on 24 September 1826.

on some days
not even a cuckoo calls
to this lone traveler[1]

leaves of sweet rush
placed on the eaves—
this smell of the spa[2]

TAGAMI KIKUSHA

---

[1] Probably inspired by Bashō's haiku:

I'm filled with sorrow—	uki ware wo
make me feel more lonely,	sabishigarase yo
cuckoo!	kankodori

[2] *Oku no hosomichi* (The narrow road to the far north) includes Bashō's haiku:

at Yamanaka	Yamanaka ya
no need for chrysanthemums—	kiku wa taoranu
this smell of the spa	yu no nioi

Bashō's verse praises the efficacy of the spa by alluding to a legendary Chinese youngster who drank dew from a chrysanthemum he found deep in the woods and lived for eight hundred years. Because leaves of sweet rush are shaped like swords, the Japanese believed in their power to drive away evil spirits and placed them on the eaves of their houses. The leaves have a strong scent, though it is different from a chrysanthemum's.

kanko sae kikanu hi mo ari hitoritabi (Hisamatsu and Imoto, vol. 16)

fukisouru noki no ayame ya yu no nioi (Ibid.)

lost in the woods—
only the sound of a leaf
falling on my hat[1]

On Mount Nikkō

not a speck of dirt
mixed with the snow this morning—
the rays of the sun[2]

[1] Written during the poet's journey to the northeast in 1781. On the way from Yamagata to Sendai, she became lost and wandered in the mountains all night long.
[2] Probably alludes to the haiku Bashō wrote on Mt. Nikkō:

how solemn!	ara tōto
green leaves, young leaves, and through them	aoba wakaba no
the rays of the sun	hi no hikari

yamanaka ya kasa ni ochiba no oto bakari (Hisamatsu and Imoto, vol. 16)

yuki ni kesa majiru chiri nashi hi no hikari (Ibid.)

Watching cormorant fishing
at the Nagara River

revealing in the dark
the sadness of things—
a fisherman's torch[1]

all things that melt
are turning verdant—
spring snow

TAGAMI KIKUSHA

---

[1] Undoubtedly echoes the haiku Bashō wrote at the Nagara River:

so exciting	omoshirōte
and, after a while, so sad—	yagate kanashiki
cormorant fishing	ubune kana

Cormorant fishing is performed at night on a boat; a fisherman manipulates a few trained cormorants to catch fish.

yami wa terasu mono no aware ya u no kagari (Hisamatsu and Imoto, vol. 16)

tokete yuku mono mina aoshi haru no yuki (Ibid.)

all the snow melts—
everywhere the fragrance
of wild plum blossoms

when a cloud parts
with the low-lying clouds
—cherry blossoms![1]

---

[1] The haiku probably echoes the famous *tanka* in *Shin kokin waka shū* by Fujiwara Teika (1162–1241):

this spring night	*haru no yo no*
the floating bridge of dreams	*yume no ukihashi*
broke off:	*todae shite*
parting with the mountaintop	*mine ni wakaruru*
low-lying clouds in the sky	*yokogumo no sora*

yuki wa mina kaori tokashite noume kana (Hisamatsu and Imoto, vol. 16)

yokogumo ni kumo wa wakarete sakura kana (Ibid.)

that first cry
was not my fancy—
a mountain cuckoo!

the moon and I
left alone—
cool on the bridge

hajime no mo soramimi de nashi hototogisu (Hisamatsu and Imoto, vol. 16)

tsuki to ware to bakari nokorinu hashisuzumi (Ibid.)

looking like clouds
only when they crumble
cloud peaks

morning glories—
in the evening, they let us
admire their buds

TAGAMI KIKUSHA

chiru toki ni kumo to miekeri kumo no mine (Hisamatsu and Imoto, vol. 16)

asagao ya yoi wa tsubomi ni tanoshimase (Ibid.)

unlikely flowers
when they bloomed—yet now
these gourds![1]

snipe on the wing—
left behind, the murmur
of a little stream[2]

---

[1] The flowers of a gourd vine are white, small, and inconspicuous.
[2] The haiku probably alludes to a well-known *tanka* in *Shin kokin waka shū* by the priest Saigyō:

even a person	*kokoro naki*
without feelings would be moved	*mi ni mo aware wa*
to this sadness	*shirarekeri*
when a snipe takes wing from the marsh	*shigi tatsu sawa no*
on the autumn nightfall	*aki no yūgure*

to wa mienu hana de atta ni fukube kana (Hisamatsu and Imoto, vol. 16)

shigi tatsu ya ato ni wa hosoki mizu no oto (Ibid.)

wild azaleas
on Mount Aso
learning how to blaze[1]

Visiting Mount Ōbaku in Uji
one year

one step outside
the temple gate, it's Japan—
a tea-picker's song[2]

[1] Written when the poet traveled to Kyushu and climbed Mt. Aso, an active volcano.
[2] The temple is Manpuku Temple in Uji, near Kyoto. Headquarters of the Ōbaku sect of Zen Buddhism, the temple was built with Ming-style architecture and so gave the impression of being in China. Uji was—and still is—famous for producing green tea.

tsutsuji bakari moe narōte ka Aso no yama (Hisamatsu and Imoto, vol. 16)

sanmon wo dereba Nihon zo chatsumiuta (Ibid.)

After visiting Yoshino Hills

on the summer hills
I saw a cloud—that's all
there was in Yoshino[1]

is this how autumn
comes to my life alone?
rainy nightfall[2]

---

[1] The haiku is accompanied by an additional note: "Someone once observed, 'Are we to look at cherry blossoms only when they are in full bloom [*Tsurezuregusa* (Essays in idleness)]?' While I agree with him, I also feel it is disappointing to see something well past its prime. On the other hand, I know someone else said, 'There is nothing you have in mind that cannot be turned into a flower [*Oi no kobumi* (The record of a travel-worn satchel)].'" Yoshino is renowned for its cherry blossoms.

[2] Written when the poet's father died, the haiku alludes to the following *tanka* in *Kokin waka shū* by Ōe Chisato:

the moon makes me muse	*tsuki mireba*
over thousands of things	*chiji ni mono koso*
that sadden my heart	*kanashikere*
even though I know autumn	*waga mi hitotsu no*
does not come to my life alone	*aki ni wa aranedo*

natsuyama ni kumo mite sumasu Yoshino kana (Hisamatsu and Imoto, vol. 16)

mi hitotsu no aki ka to zo omou ame no kure (Ibid.)

Seeing chrysanthemums in
bloom near Urin Temple

toward the white clouds
chrysanthemums by the road
breathing their scent[1]

does a dustpan
share in the Buddha's nature?
blossoms' shade[2]

[1] Urin Temple was located in Kyoto. The name of the temple literally means "cloud forest."
[2] The haiku is accompanied by the poet's drawing of a puppy sitting on a dustpan, with a broom lying nearby. The drawing alludes to a passage in the Zen classic *Mumonkan* (Gateless pass): "A monk once asked Chaochou, 'Does a puppy share in the Buddha's nature?' Chaochou answered, '*Mu*.'" Chaochou's *mu* is the No that is identical with the Yes in the deeper sphere of Zen.

shirakumo ni ka wo haku kiku no yamaji kana (Hisamatsu and Imoto, vol. 16)

chiritori ni busshō ari ya hana no kage (Ueno, *Josei haiku no sekai*)

Takeshita Shizunojo
1887–1951

Takeshita Shizunojo was one of the few women haiku poets to appear in the early years of modern Japan. Wives, at that time, were responsible for nearly all domestic matters. With a husband and five children, home life was extremely busy and oppressive for her. In 1920 she wrote

short summer night—	*mijikayo ya*
shall I throw away this baby	*chichi zeri naku ko wo*
crying for milk?	*sutechimao ka*

She included the comment: "This expresses a middle-class woman's heartfelt cry at a certain moment, when she was at a loss spiritually, physically, and materially as she was caught half by herself and half by the old customs in this transitional period."[1]

Shizunojo was born Takeshita Shizuno on 19 March 1887 on a farm in Kyushu. After finishing Fukuoka Women's Normal School, she worked as a teacher at a primary school and later as an assistant instructor at Kokura Normal School. Since she had no brother who would succeed to her father's estate, a man who later became the principal of an agricultural school was taken into her family as her husband in 1912. She became interested in haiku in 1919 and contributed to *Hototogisu* (The mountain cuckoo) the next year, but, at the time, she was unable to write the sort

---

[1] Cited in Ueno, *Josei haiku no sekai*, 75.

of haiku she wanted to write. She wanted to express herself freely, without the restrictions of *shasei* and the season words imposed by the magazine. In 1927, Takahama Kyoshi's trip to Fukuoka brought her relief, and she soon became a member of The Mountain Cuckoo circle. Her husband died suddenly in 1934. She subsequently had to take a job as a librarian at Fukuoka Municipal Library. In 1937 she helped form the Students' Haiku League, gathering haiku-loving students from Tokyo, Kyushu, and other universities. Its magazine, *Seisōken* (The stratosphere), was under her son's editorship. She lived to see the publication of the only book of her haiku: *Hayate* (The gusty wind). It came out in 1940 and included 335 works. After the war, despite a chronic kidney condition, she cultivated small parcels of land to help feed her mother and children. She died on 3 August 1951. *Takeshita Shizunojo kubun shū* (The collected haiku and prose of Takeshita Shizunojo) was brought out in 1964.

all night long
a woman asleep
like a silkworm

gloves off my hands—
on the pearl of the ring
a thin cloud

yo nagaki me kaiko no gotoku ine ireri (Tomiyasu et al., vol. 3)

tebukuro toru ya yubiwa no tama no usugumori (Ibid.)

the more callouses
the more brightly
my ring sparkles

                              the New Year, yet still
                              that same old winter hat—
                              my big husband

TAKESHITA SHIZUNOJO

mame fuete masumasu hikaru yubiwa kana (Tomiyasu et al., vol. 3)

kotoshi nao sono fuyubōshi sodaizuma (Ibid.)

in the rain and wind
uttering no cry
a shrike in winter

no longer seeking
the sun, a magnificent
sunflower[1]

---

[1] It has become the time for sunflowers to bear seeds. Because the poem was written in 1930, the sunflower may stand for the poet, who had regained confidence in haiku.

ame kaze ni mokumoku to shite mozu no fuyu (Tomiyasu et al., vol. 3)

hi wo owanu ōhimawari to narinikeri (Ibid.)

my husband gone —
flakes of spring snow
out of a blue sky[1]

            seashells on the table
            concealing the melodies
            of the deep sea

TAKESHITA SHIZUNOJO

[1] One of several haiku written shortly after 25 January 1933, when the poet's husband suddenly died of a brain hemorrhage.

tsuma yuku to seiten haru no yuki wo furu (Ueno, *Kindai no joryū haiku*)

taku no kai shinkai no fu wo hiso to himu (Tomiyasu et al., vol. 3)

the round sun
and the slender moon
with a paper kite

the library at dusk—
playing in the spring twilight
elves out of the books

maruki hi to nagaki tsuki ari tako no sora (Tomiyasu et al., vol. 3)

shoko kurashi yūbe oboro no shoma asobu (Ueno, *Kindai no joryū haiku*)

inhaling urban dust
and turning it into flesh
a May carp[1]

                                    those dumb menfolks
                                    smelling of sweat
                                    —I go and join them

---

[1] A May carp is a carp-shaped banner hoisted outside the home on 5 May, Boys' Festival Day, by a family with a little boy. A carp, one of the most vigorous fish, symbolizes health and strength.

kōjin wo sūte shishi to su satsukigoi (Tomiyasu et al., vol. 3)

ase kusaki noro no otoko no mure ni gosu (Ibid.)

a pittance
is what I earn, along with
frequent heat rash

unconcerned
with the tenant farmers' dispute
rice plants have grown

TAKESHITA SHIZUNOJO

sokubaku no zeni wo ete eshi asebo wa mo (Tomiyasu et al., vol 3)

kosaku sōgi ni kakawari mo naku ine to naru (Ibid.)

fire on the mountains—
between heaven and earth
darkness as ever

On an October day, I saw
off a friend who has been
drafted because of the war
with China

autumn rain comes
making his heavy uniform
even heavier

sanka moyu kenkon no yami ni yurugi naku (Tomiyasu et al., vol. 3)

shūu kinu omoki seii wo omokarashime (Ibid.)

in the mosquito's
buzz, a thread of thought
begins in my mind

stubbornly
refusing to buy a diary
this woman

ka no koe no naka ni shisaku no ito wo eshi (Tomiyasu et al., vol. 3)

katakuna ni nikki wo kawanu onna nari (Ibid.)

grief and anger—
I spit out black, black
watermelon seeds

Cowherd shining in the sky—
on the earth, a woman bowed
under a pack of food[1]

---

[1] Written on 7 July 1949. According to legend, 7 July is the only night of the year when two heavenly lovers, the Cowherd (Altair) and the Weaver Maiden (Vega), are allowed to meet. Four years after the end of the war, there was still a severe shortage of food in urban areas.

hifun ari hakishi suika no shushi kuroku (Tomiyasu et al., vol. 3)

ten ni kengyū chi ni onna ite kate wo ou (Ueno, *Kindai no joryū haiku*)

Sugita Hisajo
1890–1946

"Devoted to art, I have not taken good care of my home," Sugita Hisajo wrote. "I am nothing as a woman. A vampire. A heretic. I have always been accused, pressured, and spat upon this way by people around me, so that I thought of suicide several times."[1] These words, from the preface to her own magazine *Hanagoromo* (Clothes for flower viewing), well suggest her attitude toward writing haiku. Passionate and idealistic, she worked hard to compose haiku while neglecting domestic chores. Such conflict between ideals and reality was to plague her throughout her adult life.

Hisajo was born Akabori Hisa on 30 May 1890 in Kagoshima, Kyushu. Her father, a government official, moved to Okinawa and later to Taiwan, where she finished primary school. She then enrolled in Ochanomizu Girls' Middle School in Tokyo. Shortly after graduation she married Sugita Unai, a son of an illustrious family; he taught art at Kokura Middle School in Kyushu. Two daughters were soon born. She learned haiku from her older brother in 1915 and developed a great admiration for Takahama Kyoshi. Her haiku progressed rapidly, but her husband disappointed her by being an art teacher, not an artist. In 1920 she contracted a kidney disease and had to live in Tokyo for a year, during which time she contemplated divorce. She relented, however, and was soon after baptised as a Methodist, her church-related activities lasting for several

[1] Cited in Iida et al., eds., *Kanshō gendai haiku zenshū*, 8:30.

years. Her best years as a haiku poet followed. In 1932 she was made a member of The Mountain Cuckoo circle and started her own magazine, *Hanagoromo*. Suddenly in 1936, however, Kyoshi expelled her and two others from membership without giving any reasons. Since the other two were critical of Kyoshi's objectives, they and the group's other members understood their expulsion, but Hisajo had been wholeheartedly loyal to Kyoshi and was utterly surprised by his action. She was crestfallen, and she gradually abandoned haiku. She died on 21 January 1946, at a sanitarium near Fukuoka. *Sugita Hisajo kushū* (The collected haiku of Sugita Hisajo) was assembled posthumously in 1952. Her life has been dealt with by various writers, including Yoshiya Nobuko (1896–1973), Matsumoto Seichō (1909–1992), and Akimoto Matsuyo (1911–2001).[2]

---

[2] Yoshiya, *Soko no nuketa hishaku* (1964); Matsumoto, "Kiku makura," *Bungei shunjū* (August 1953); Akimoto, *Yama hototogisu hoshii mama* (1966).

spring cold—
round a young chrysanthemum leaf
how sharp the teeth!

at spring dawn
unforgetful of a dream
long eyelashes

harusamu ya kizami surudoki kogiku no me (Tomiyasu et al., vol. 9)

shungyō no yume no ato ou nagamatsuge (Ibid.)

gums itching
the baby bites my nipple—
spring's hazy sky

                              my child with a cold—
                              her forelocks almost
                              reach her eyebrows

haguki kayuku chikubi kamu ko ya hanagumori (Tomiyasu et al., vol. 9)

kaze no ko ya mayu ni nobi kishi hitaigami (Ibid.)

reading the Bible
this loneliness—
rain on the blossoms

home from blossom-viewing—
as I disrobe, many straps
cling to my body[1]

SUGITA HISAJO

[1] Written in 1919. Kyoshi said at the time that this was a woman's haiku that no man could imitate. Hisajo spoke of the boldness through which the complex beauty of colors was expressed aesthetically.

baibaru wo yomu sabishisa yo hana no ame (Tomiyasu et al., vol. 9)

hanagoromo nugu ya matsuwaru himo iroiro (Ibid.)

a goldbug crawling
in the shade of leaves —
gusty rain

haiku poet,
caring mother —
this summer I'm a wreck

SUGITA HISAJO

koganemushi hakage wo ayumu fūu kana (Tomiyasu et al., vol. 9)

hoku no ware jibo taru ware ya natsu yasenu (Ibid.)

in a moonflower bud
just beginning to open
deep creases

lotuses in bloom—
on my cheeks the morning sun
isn't yet warm

yūgao ya hiraki kakarite hida fukaku (Tomiyasu et al., vol. 9)

hasu saku ya asahi mada hō ni atsukarazu (Ibid.)

sewing in the lamplight
I teach spelling to my child—
autumn rain

my parasol's shadow
makes the wild chrysanthemums
look darker

hi ni nūte ko ni oshiyuru ji aki no ame (Tomiyasu et al., vol. 9)

waga kasa no kage no naka koki nogiku kana (Ibid.)

reading a play
dishes left in the sink
this winter night

she mends socks
not quite a Nora
this teacher's wife[1]

---

[1] Written in 1922. Ibsen's play *A Doll's House* was popular among educated women in Japan at around this time.

gikyoku yomu fuyu yo no shokki tsukeshi mama (Tomiyasu et al., vol. 9)

tabi tsugu ya Nora to mo narazu kyōshizuma (Ibid.)

hardly a word spoken
the man and his wife part—
autumn nightfall

morning glories—
smog begins to foul
the town's sky

kotoba sukunaku wakareshi fūfu aki no yoi (Tomiyasu et al., vol. 9)

asagao ya nigori sometaru machi no sora (Ibid.)

my illness ebbs—
propped by a wrecked boat
I bathe in the sun

to the dark Buddha
amid the scent of chrysanthemums
I offer this candle

SUGITA HISAJO

byōkan ya hasen ni motare hinataboko (Tomiysau et al., vol. 9)

kiku no ka no kuraki hotoke ni hi wo kenzu (Ibid.)

air-raid sirens—
the last to turn off the lights
is a temple with blossoms

                              chasing a butterfly
                              deep into the spring woods
                              I am lost

SUGITA HISAJO

kūshū no hi wo keshi okure hana no tera (Tomiyasu et al., vol. 9)

chō ōte haruyama fukaku mayoikeri (Ibid.)

Hashimoto Takako
1899–1963

As a young woman, Hashimoto Takako had beauty, talent, and affluence. Yet her husband died when she was still in her prime, and the social reorganization resulting from the Second World War took away most of the advantages she had enjoyed. "Between one person and another, there is no bridge,"[1] she is reported to have said. Through haiku, she tried hard to build these bridges until the end of her life. Whether she succeeded in that attempt remains a question, but her haiku grew progressively richer.

Born as Yamatani Tama in Tokyo on 15 January 1899, Takako majored in painting at Kikusaka Women's School of Art, but because of ill health she did not graduate. In 1917 she married Hashimoto Toyojirō, an architect who had studied in the United States. Their house in Kokura, Kyushu, was a local center of cultural activities, visited by a number of prominent poets, artists, and musicians. Takahama Kyoshi, along with Sugita Hisajo, was there in 1922, which gave Takako the impetus to start writing haiku. Hisajo became her initial teacher. They had to separate in 1929, however, when Takako and her family moved to Osaka. In 1935 she made Yamaguchi Seishi her new mentor. After Toyojirō's death two years later, haiku became her only emotional resource. She moved to the rural area of Nara in 1944 and devoted herself to haiku composition. Her books of haiku appeared one after another: *Umi tsubame*

[1] Cited in Iida et al., eds., *Kanshō gendai haiku zenshū*, 8:209.

(Sea swallows) in 1944, *Shinano* (The province of Shinano) in 1947, and *Beniito* (The red thread) in 1951. She travelled widely and engaged in many activities that promoted haiku, founding the magazine *Shichiyō* (Seven days) in 1948. In 1959 she was awarded the Nara Cultural Prize. She died on 29 May 1963 of liver cancer; her last collection of haiku, *Myōjū* (The end of life), was published soon after. *Hashimoto Takako zen kushū* (The complete haiku of Hashimoto Takako) appeared in 1973.

the typhoon passes—
quietly asleep
a man near death[1]

a flowering chestnut
falls, the sound assailing me
as I stand

---

[1] Written in 1937. "A man near death" was the poet's husband.

taifū sugishi shizukani inete shi ni chikaki (Hashimoto)

hanaguri no kiraruru oto wo mi ni shi tatsu (Ibid.)

mother and child
play cards, while a fox
cries at night

taking up chopsticks
I am all alone—
it snows and snows

HASHIMOTO TAKAKO

haha to ko no toranpu kitsune naku yo nari (Hashimoto)

hashi toru toki hata to hitori ya yuki furi furu (Ibid.)

plucked
feathers of a fowl
under the cold moon

to the cold moon
the bonfire goes up in one flame
after another

mushiritaru ichiwa no umō kangekka (Hashimoto)

kangetsu ni takibi hitohira zutsu noboru (Ibid.)

to the starlit sky
apples overflowing
from the storehouse

wisteria plumes
as long as they can bear it
hold the rain

HASHIMOTO TAKAKO

hoshizora e mise yori ringo afure ori (Hashimoto)

fujibusa no tauru kagiri no ame fukumu (Ibid.)

the baby carriage
and the wild waves
side by side in summer

in the sweltering sky
a ladder—someone carries it
to the deep shade

HASHIMOTO TAKAKO

ubaguruma natsu no dotō ni yoko muki ni (Hashimoto)

enten no hashigo kuraki ni katsugi iru (Ibid.)

at one place
it goes through darkness—
the ring of dancers

a flash of lightning
coming from the north, I look
to the north

hito tokoro kuraki wo kuguru odori no wa (Hashimoto)

inabikari kita yori sureba kita wo miru (Ibid.)

the fierce snowfall—
I'll die, having known no hands
other than my husband's

washed hair—
in the same sunlight
a bee is dead

yuki hageshi tsuma no te no hoka shirazu shisu (Hashimoto)

araigami onaji hinata ni hachi shishite (Ibid.)

my hair is not yet dry—
in the distance hangs the shed skin
of a snake

                          looking downwards
                          the smell of my own breath
                          in the snowy field

kami kawakazu tōku ni hebi no kinu kakaru (Hashimoto)

utsumuku toki ono ga iki no ka yukino nite (Ibid.)

one moon
and one frozen lake
sparkling at each other

a heron is shot!
feathers, like scattering blossoms,
come falling down

tsuki ichirin iteko ichirin hikari au (Hashimoto)

shigi utaru umō no sange okure furu (Ibid.)

having eaten a lizard
how carefully the cat
licks its own body!

on a snowy day
my bathed body, a finger
a toe—I love all of it[1]

[1] Written the day before she was admitted to the hospital for the last time.

tokage kui neko nengoro ni mi wo nameru (Hashimoto)

yuki no hi no yokushin isshi isshi itoshi (Ibid.)

Mitsuhashi Takajo
1899–1972

Mitsuhashi Takajo said: "To write a haiku is to remove a scale. Doing so is proof that we are alive."[1] She herself was covered with "scales": that is, by fragments of the complex self she had constructed to protect herself. From her youth onwards, her haiku embraced a wide variety of topics and styles, until the grief of old age, the wish for transfiguration, and forebodings of death came largely to occupy her work. The unevenness of her work indicates a determination for self-improvement whatever the poetic cost.

Takajo was born Mitsuhashi Takako on 24 December 1899 in Nara, the daughter of a government official who was also a *tanka* poet. As a young girl, she followed her father in writing *tanka*, but when she married in 1922, she began learning haiku, which her husband, a dentist, was fond of writing himself. After the Great Tokyo Earthquake of 1923, the family moved to Tokyo and opened a dental clinic. Takajo began submitting haiku to newspaper columns, and her work improved. She joined a group of poets who founded *Kon* (The dark blue) in 1936, but it ceased publication a couple of years later. In 1940 she published the collection of haiku *Himawari* (Sunflowers), and the next year she brought out *Uo no hire* (The fish's fins), the former mainly describing her outward life and the latter often hinting at her inner feelings. The tumultous war years and their aftermath, during which her only son was

---

[1] Cited in Iida et al., eds., *Kanshō gendai haiku zenshū*, 8:268.

sent to the front and her husband fell gravely ill from overwork, were recorded in *Hakkotsu* (The bleached bones), her third collection, which appeared in 1952. The following year she joined some avant-garde poets in bringing out *Bara* (Roses) and its sequel *Haiku hyōron* (Haiku criticism), both progressive magazines that allowed experimental haiku. These new ventures, which included abstract haiku with space in midcourse, were collected in *Shida jigoku* (The fern hell) in 1961. Her last book of haiku, *Buna* (Beeches), was published in 1970. She must have been aware of her approaching death, for many of the poems in it show a sense of mortality. She had been in poor health for the previous six years or so; she died on 7 April 1972. *Mitsuhashi Takajo zen kushū* (The complete haiku of Mitsuhashi Takajo) came out in 1976.

heaven and earth
suddenly changing places—
falling ill in autumn

climb this tree
and you'll be a she-devil—
red leaves in the sunset glow

tenchi futo sakashima ni ari aki wo yamu (Mitsuhashi)

kono ki noboraba kijo to naru beshi yūmomiji (Ibid.)

cannas in bloom—
eat that crimson, and you'll burn
to death

up on a hydro pole
the electrician turns
into a cicada

kanna ano beni kuinaba inochi yake shinan (Mitsuhashi)

denchū ni noborite kōfu semi to naru (Ibid.)

autumn wind—
more transparent than water
fins of a fish

a woman stands
all alone, ready to wade
across the Milky Way

akikaze ya mizu yori awaki uo no hire (Mitsuhashi)

onna hitori tateri ginga wo wataru beku (Ibid.)

the southerly wind
becoming a peacock
challenges death

even on a day
when heaven and earth are still
ants hurry onwards

MITSUHASHI TAKAJO

nanpū no kujaku to narite shi ni idomu (Mitsuhashi)

ametsuchi no shizukanaru hi mo ari isogu (Ibid.)

      the balloon
      filled with sorrow
      rising upwards

falling leaves
falling leaves falling leaves

falling on my bed too[1]

---

[1] An example of the poet's free-verse haiku, which are not restricted by the 5-7-5 syllable pattern.

kanashibi no michite fūsen maiagaru (Mitsuhashi)

ochiba ochiba ochiba fushido no naka ni mo furu (Ibid.)

ivy having died
the entire trunk
inextricably bound

winter has begun—
trees alive and dead
indistinguishable

tsuta karete isshin ganjigarame nari (Mitsuhashi)

fuyu ni iru miwake gataki wa kareki to shiki (Ibid.)

toward thin ice
my shadow moves, moves
till it's drowned

their lives last
only while aflame—

a woman and a pepper pod

hakuhyō e waga kage yukite dekishi seri (Mitsuhashi)

moyuru ma ga inochi onna to tōgarashi (Ibid.)

a graveyard—
the camellia wanting to fall
as soon as it blooms

the old warbler
when tears fill its eyes
lets out a cry

hakahara ya tsubaki saku yori chiritagaru (Mitsuhashi)

rōō ya namida tamareba nakinikeri (Ibid.)

where the turtle
has gone down, a dimple
floats on the water

the aged person
wanting to become a tree
embraces a tree

kame shizumu mizu ni ekubo wo ukabete wa (Mitsuhashi)

sue wa ki ni naritai rōjin ki wo idaki (Ibid.)

under an oak tree
father and mother playing
hide and seek[1]

among thousands
of singing insects, one
singing out of tune

[1] This haiku and the next were found in the poet's notebook after her death.

donguri no juka chichi haha no kakurenbo (Mitsuhashi)

sen no mushi naku ippiki no kuruinaki (Ibid.)

Ishibashi Hideno
1909–1947

Sakura koku (Cherry blossoms deep), published in 1949 by her husband Yamamoto Kenkichi, is the only book authored by Ishibashi Hideno. The contents were originally selected by Hideno and were edited by her husband after her death. The book includes twelve essays and some 260 haiku. "I actually feel," said Yamamoto, "that haiku began with Bashō and ended with Hideno."[1] Certainly, her death was a devastating blow to Yamamoto, but there is more than a little truth in his judgment. *Sakura koku* was the first recipient of the Kawabata Bōsha Prize, which became one of the highest honors in haiku.

Born Yabu Hideno in Nara on 19 February 1909, Hideno started writing haiku in emulation of her elder sister when she was twelve or thirteen years old. Having gone to Tokyo and enrolled in the secondary division of the prestigious Bunka Gakuin School, she learned haiku from Takahama Kyoshi and *tanka* from Yosano Akiko (1878–1942). The school's college division did not teach haiku as a course, so when she graduated to that level, she persuaded Kyoshi to critique her writing in his spare time. She was married in 1929, but her first nine years of marriage were so tempestuous that she did not write haiku. Then in 1938 she began attending the novelist Yokomitsu Riichi's (1898–1947) haiku meetings, which revived her interest in the form. In 1945, after she had given birth to a baby girl, she accompanied

---

[1] Cited in Tomiyasu et al., eds., *Gendai haiku taikei*, 7:351.

her husband to Matsue, a city on the coast of the Sea of Japan. It was there that tuberculosis, which she had contracted some time before, slowly began to show its symptoms. A year later her husband got a job as a newspaper reporter in Kyoto, where she and her child joined him. Her tuberculosis got worse, and no effective medicine was available to treat it. She struggled to write haiku, though she suffered a great deal from her illness and from postwar scarcities. She died on 26 September 1947, at a sanitarium outside Kyoto.

the winter-blooming plum—
buds touching one another
in the twilight

the mantis
crawling on the ground
snarls at the ground

kanbai ya tsubomi fureau hono akari (Ishibashi)

tōrō no chi wo haeba chi ni ikarikeri (Ibid.)

cicadas at nightfall—
every face passes by
without speaking a word

snake's tail—
all things on the hillside
hush their voice

yūzemi ya dono kao mo mono iwade yuku (Ishibashi)

hebi no o ya yamasaka mono no koe hisome (Ibid.)

Air raids night after night

clear starlit sky
in freezing night, after the planes'
roar has vanished

Soldier of a defeated
country

autumn's hot sun —
nowhere on his military cap
twinkle the stars[1]

---

[1] After the end of the war, some former Japanese soldiers would wear army caps after stripping off the stars that showed their rank.

hoshi sumeba kan'ya no kion sude ni naku (Ishibashi)

aki atsushi seishō sude ni naki bō ni (Ibid.)

Often seen in the street

to a redhead
"Hello!"—how depressing
this spring rain![1]

mosses in bloom—
the Buddha fading away
from the stone's surface

[1] Hungry Japanese children, when they saw Occupation Army soldiers in the street, would call out to them in English, hoping to receive some chocolate or chewing gum.

kōmō ni harou utateki haru no ame (Ishibashi)

koke saku ya hotoke usururu ishi no omo (Ibid.)

that ailing leaf
fallen into an eddy—
how fast it floats away!

departing autumn—
water feels softer
in the mouth

wakuraba no uzu ni nori yuku hayasa kana (Ishibashi)

yuku aki ya fukumite mizu no yawarakaki (Ibid.)

the leaves have fallen—
a panhandler
with no age

Self-derision

chapped hands
and no rice—I weep
with a monkey's face[1]

---

[1] The haiku was written in 1947 when there was a severe shortage of food in Japan.

ochiba shite katai ni yowai nakarikeri (Ishibashi)

akagari ya ii hori nakeba saru no kao (Ibid.)

in the chilling wind
hands of a woman
splitting a fish's belly

at spring dawn
something I've spat out
gleams serenely

kaze saete uo no hara saku onna no te (Ishibashi)

shungyō no waga haku mono no hikari sumu (Ibid.)

to a daddy longlegs
my feverish hand extends
for no reason at all

one naked baby
is all I've got
and I pray

ISHIBASHI HIDENO

gaganbo ni netsu no te wo nobe rachi mo nashi (Ishibashi)

hadakago wo hitori eshi nomi reihai su (Ibid.)

glorious sunset—
feeling a chill, my teeth,
twenty in all, rattle

the fiery moon
rises, the fireworks show
having come to an end

ISHIBASHI HIDENO

ōyūyake okan ni narasu ha nijūmai (Ishibashi)

hi no yōna tsuki no de hanabi uchi owaru (Ibid.)

the summer moon —
my lungs keep crumbling
while I am asleep

shrill cicadas drum like rain —
my child can't catch up
with the wheelchair[1]

---

[1] Written on 21 July 1947 when the poet was admitted to a sanitarium for the last time. Her daughter was then three years old. This was Hideno's last haiku, since her doctors prohibited her from writing in the sanitarium.

natsu no tsuki hai kuetsutsu mo nemuru naru (Ishibashi)

semi shigure ko wa tansōsha ni oitsukezu (Ibid.)

Katsura Nobuko
b. 1914

Katsura Nobuko was born Niwa Nobuko in Osaka on 1 November 1914 and almost died of acute pneumonia when she was five. After graduating from Ōtemae Girls' High School, she began writing haiku when the poems in *Kikan* (The flagship) magazine impressed her with their nontraditional style. She subsequently met the magazine's editor, Hino Sōjō, and became his protégé. Her marriage in 1939 changed her family name to Katsura, but her husband died two years later. Childless, she returned to her mother's home. On 13 March 1945, American planes bombed Osaka. Nobuko's house caught fire. She struggled in vain to douse the flames. Her mother was nowhere to be seen. Nobuko was just able to gather her haiku manuscripts before fleeing barefooted from the fire. Finally, when the danger had passed, she was reunited with her mother. "You are safe—that's all I care," her mother said, weeping. The rescued manuscripts were later published in her first volume, *Gekkō shō* (Beams of the moon, 1949).

After she had worked at the library of the Kobe College of Commerce for two years, Nobuko settled into a secretarial job at Kinki Vehicles Company in 1946, and she remained there until her retirement in 1970. In 1954 she helped Katō Chiyoko edit the magazine *Josei haiku* (Women's haiku), becoming one of the most faithful participants in its meetings. After *Gekkō shō*, she published *Nyoshin* (The female body) in 1955, *Banshun* (Late spring) in 1967, *Shinryoku* (Young leaves) in 1974, and several other collections. In 1970 she founded the magazine *Sōen* (The grass garden), which is still publishing today. Her honors include the Women's Prize in Modern Haiku in 1977, the Osaka Cultural and Artistic Award in 1981, and the Dakotsu Prize in 1992, the last being the most prestigious prize in haiku, established in 1966 to honor Iida Dakotsu (1885–1962). Her ninth collection of haiku, *Kaei* (The shadows of flowers), came out in 1996.

                    the woman at high noon
                    untiringly watches
                    a distant fire

Christmas—
since when? this sadness
of being a wife

KATSURA NOBUKO

hiru no onna tōkaji akazu nagamekeri (Katsura, *Gekkō shō*)

Kurisumasu tsuma no kanashimi itsu shika mochi (Ibid.)

women's hearts
touch one another—hanging
plumes of wisteria

evening cherry blossoms—
the faces looking up
grow dusky too

KATSURA NOBUKO

onna no kokoro fureōte ite fuji taruru (Katsura, *Gekkō shō*)

yūzakura miaguru kao mo kurenikeri (Ibid.)

wild geese—
between their cries, a slice
of silence

loosely dressed
I meet with somebody
this night of fireflies

karigane no shizukasa wo hedate hedate naku (Katsura, *Gekkō shō*)

yuruyaka ni kite hito to au hotaru no yo (Ibid.)

with nothing
to touch, a dead branch
grabs at the sky

with two breasts
between my shoulders, and this gloom—
season rain without end

KATSURA NOBUKO

fururu mono nakute kareeda sora ni hari (Katsura, Nyoshin)

futokoro ni chibusa aru usa tsuyu nagaki (Ibid.)

though it flies and flies
the wild goose cannot escape
from the moon's rays

on the scale
my bathed and steaming body
this night of snow

KATSURA NOBUKO

tobedo tobedo kari gekkō wo nogare ezu (Katsura, Nyoshin)

yuagari no mi wo nose yuki no yo no hakari (Ibid.)

beyond the dark
where I disrobe
an iris in bloom

snow on the window—
a female body makes hot water
overflow the tub

i wo nugishi yami no anata ni ayame saku (Katsura, *Nyoshin*)

mado no yuki nyotai nite yu wo afureshimu (Ibid.)

on the skin of a woman
who has never conceived
hot autumn sun

the first day of spring—
a wind from the ocean
but no ocean in sight

migomorishi koto nashi hada ni akibi atsushi (Katsura, *Nyoshin*)

risshun no umi yori no kaze umi miezu (Katsura, *Banshun*)

on the water
a clear image of blossoms

death close by[1]

                                        in my native town
                                        a summer tree, its top
                                        pointed like a sword

---

[1] "Death" is close by, because the mirror image of the cherry blossoms, clearer than the actual flowers, will disappear with the slightest breath of wind.

mizu ni utsuru hana no kokumei shi wa soko ni (Katsura, *Banshun*)

furusato ni kissaki wo motsu natsuki ari (Katsura, *Shinryoku*)

the grass roots
extending to the sleep
of a snake

think of the burning fire
at the bottom of the earth
last year, this year

KATSURA NOBUKO

kusa no ne no hebi no nemuri ni todokikeri (Katsura, *Juei*)

chi no soko no moyuru to omoe kozo kotoshi (Ibid.)

a bamboo shoot
taking off its sheath —
for a moment, no wind

the cry of water
in the dark, a beast's eyes
then fireflies

take kawa wo nugu hitotoki no mufū kana (Haiku, September 1995)

mizuoto no yami ni kemono no me to hotaru (Haiku, September 1996)

Yoshino Yoshiko
b. 1915

Yoshino Yoshiko lives in Matsuyama, a city well known in Japan for haiku. Masaoka Shiki, Takahama Kyoshi, and Nakamura Kusatao all wrote haiku there when they were young. The Shiki Memorial Museum, which honors the poet and his circle, is one of the finest devoted to him. In 2000, the International Haiku Convention was held in Matsuyama, and awards named after Shiki were presented. Activities like this are common in Matsuyama, and Yoshiko has long been part of that tradition.

She was born in Taiwan on 13 July 1915, the daughter of Ogawa Naoyoshi, who was a friend of Shiki's, a professor of linguistics, and a leading expert on the Taiwanese language. Two months after her birth, Yoshiko's maternal uncle adopted her and took her to Matsuyama. As a young girl she wrote free verse. In 1933 her studies in English literature at Dōshisha Women's University were interrupted by marriage. She bore one son and three daughters. She began writing haiku seriously in 1947 under the guidance of Ōno Rinka (1904–1984) and published them in his magazine *Hama* (Seashore) the next year. Her first book of haiku, *Kurenai* (The crimson), appeared in 1956. Somehow, in addition to bringing up her children, she found time for many activities related to haiku. Her second and third books, *Hatsuarashi* (The first storm) and *Tsurumai* (The dance of the crane), were published in 1971 and 1976. In 1979 she started the haiku magazine *Hoshi* (Stars), which still publishes. She has traveled widely, going not only to various places in Japan but also to Europe, North America, Africa, and China, and she has attended many international conferences such as the U.S.–Japan Haiku Conference in San Francisco in 1987, the World Poets' Conference in Bangkok in 1988, and the Japan–China Symposia on Fixed Verse in Peking and Shanghai in 1989. In 1987 the Ehime Prefectural Government honored her for her contributions in haiku. Her latest volume, *Ryūsui* (Flowing water), came out in 2000.

though dead
the chrysanthemum does not fall—
a horrid sight to see

their mom being ill
children do not fight—
cold supper for them!

YOSHINO YOSHIKO

karete nao kiku chirazaru wo nikumikeri (Yoshino, *Yoshino Yoshiko shū*)

waga yameba kora isakawanu yūge samushi (Ibid.)

thin ice
and trapped beneath it
the sunset glow

 a man enters
 the room, disturbing the scent
 of daffodils

YOSHINO YOSHIKO

usurai no ura ni yūyake komorikeri (Yoshino, *Yoshino Yoshiko shū*)

otoko kite heya nuchi suisen no nioi midaru (Ibid.)

large sunflowers
surround the house
of a tall family

snow-capped mountains,
rough waves, and between them
a long freight train

ōhimawari megurashi kazoku mina chōshin (Yoshino, *Yoshino Yoshiko shū*)

setsurei to gekirō no aida kasha nagashi (Ibid.)

as if mending
socks, I repair my mind
and live on

hazy moonlit night—
a stream, purling in Japanese,
makes me feel at home[1]

[1] Written during the poet's visit to Yosemite National Park in 1974.

tabi tsugu goto kokoro tsukuroi tsutsu iku mo (Yoshino, *Yoshino Yoshiko shū*)

kiritsukiyo mioto wo wago no yasuragi ni (Ibid.)

ill on a journey
I'm fearful of silence
this winter nightfall

like a ninja
a crow on the paddy
always alone

tabi ni yami buin ni obiyu fuyu no kure (Yoshino, *Kashin*)

ninja meku shirota no karasu itsumo ichiwa (Ibid.)

peace of mind, like
floating in the womb, this bath
on a New Year's morning

the bamboo plant
shedding its sheath
in front of women

taisui ni uku yasukesa no hatsuyu kana (Yoshino, *Kashin*)

take kawa wo nugu onna-ra no kakomu naka (Ibid.)

the sound of white plates
clinking together —
a night in autumn

on the snowfield
forever parallel
tracks of a cart

shirasara no fureau oto no yoru no aki (Yoshino, *Kashin*)

setsugen ya majiwarazu shite wadachiato (Ibid.)

like a woman
collapsing, the white lotus
has fallen full length

on the hilltop
someone hammering a stake
to awaken the hill

onna kuzururu goto hakuren no chirinikeri (Yoshino, *Kashin*)

sanchō ni kui uchite yama mezameshimu (Ibid.)

like a deserted
child, a spray of blossoms
in an old tree

how dreadful!
every mask in the *noh* drama
has its mouth open[1]

---

[1] The *noh* drama uses masks for its main characters. Every mask, whether it is a god's, a demon's, or a man's, has its mouth open.

wasurego no goto rōkan ni hana hitofusa (Yoshino, Ryūsui)

susamaji ya nōomote mina kuchi hiraki (Ibid.)

on the water
staring at its own image—
a stray goose

                                                 light of the moon
                                                 amassed in the crater—
                                               snowy Mount Fuji

mizu no mo no shi ga kage miiru haguregamo (Yoshino, *Ryūsui*)

gekkō wo kakō ni tamete yuki no Fuji (Ibid.)

Tsuda Kiyoko
b. 1920

When young, Tsuda Kiyoko wrote nothing but *tanka*. But one day she happened to attend one of Hashimoto Takako's haiku meetings, at which most of the participants were men who seemed to pay little attention to their appearance. Asked to present a haiku, Kiyoko had no seventeen-syllable verse ready; instead she offered the first half of a *tanka*. It was a novel "haiku," so novel that it was accepted by Takako. The experience opened Kiyoko's eyes to this new verse form, and she began experimenting with it. Takako became her teacher.

Tsuda Kiyoko was born on 25 June 1920 in a farmhouse in the rural part of Nara Prefecture. After graduating from Nara Women's Normal School, she served as a primary school teacher in Nara and Osaka, holding the latter job until her retirement in 1976. She has never married. Besides Takako, she acknowledges Yamaguchi Seishi as her teacher. Seishi's magazine, *Tenrō* (The heavenly wolf), awarded her its highest prize in 1951, and her first volume of haiku, *Raihai* (Worship), came out in 1959. In 1967 she founded Gathering Clouds, a haiku circle, with Seishi and a group of friends. In 1971 she started the magazine *Sara* (The sala tree), which lasted until 1986. She took a trip to Alaska in 1973, and her second book of haiku, *Nininshō* (The second person), was published the same year. Her third collection, *Jūsō* (Mountain-range traversing), came out in 1982. In the meantime, she had been invited to lecture by various institutions, including Japan Broadcasting Company. Her travels have taken her as far as China and Africa; she is interested in such out-of-the-way destinations as deserts, glaciers, and the Silk Road. After *Sara* ended, she started *Kei* (K), which still continues to publish. In 2000 her latest book, *Muhō* (No directions), received the Dakotsu Prize.

with a young child
shaking a tree
the house in summer

a pure maiden
eating a watermelon
smells of steel

ki wo yusaburu ko ga ite natsu no ie to naru (Tsuda, *Raihai*)

maotome ya suika wo hameba hagane no ka (Ibid.)

from moment to moment
I live, stretching both hands
to the bonfire

long rain in the ruins—
a headless apostle
hands still at prayer[1]

---

[1] This haiku and the next were written in 1954, when the poet traveled to Nagasaki and visited a Catholic church destroyed by the atomic bomb.

setsuna setsuna ni iku takibi ni wa ryōte dashi (Tsuda, *Raihai*)

haikyo ni tsuyu kubi naki shito no te ga inoru (Ibid.)

starving spider
between tree and cross
goes back and forth

the rose garden—
unless you retrace your steps
there's no exit

kumo uete ki to takuzō wo yukiki seru (Tsuda, *Raihai*)

bara no sono hiki kaesaneba deguchi nashi (Ibid.)

heavy with honey
below the belt, a bee
confronts an enemy

amnesia—
beneath the jellyfish's dome
the sea

hara ni mitsu omokushite hachi teki to au (Tsuda, *Raihai*)

kioku sōshitsu kurage no kasa no naka no umi (Ibid.)

hunter and wild geese
on the same lake
wait for daybreak

wintering butterfly,
the moor as drained
as any mother

TSUDA KIYOKO   163

ryōfu to kamo onaji kojō ni yoake matsu (Tsuda, Raihai)

fuyu kosu chō arechi wa haha no gotoku yasu (Ibid.)

not knowing
the height of the mountain
an ant crawls on my knee

over the frozen field
an eagle comes, its hungry eyes
upon my flesh

yama no takasa shirazu ni ari wa hiza wo hau (Tsuda, Nininshō)

hyōgen ni washi kite ware no namami horu (Iida et al., Kanshō gendai haiku zenshū, vol. 11)

flying across the dunes
a butterfly and a crow
each without company

tree leaves fall
as if visited by death
each at a different time

sakyū tobu chō mo karasu mo tsure wa nashi (Iida et al., *Kanshō gendai haiku zenshū*, vol. 11)

ki no ha chiru betsubetsu ni shi ga kuru gotoku (Tsuda, *Jūsō*)

the school is filled
with voices, while the universe
loads up with snow

a flying beetle
its wings invisible
its speed plain to see

gakkō ni koe michi yuki wa chū ni michi (Tsuda, *Kuzugoromo*)

kabutomushi tobu hane miezu hayasa miyu (Tsuda, *Nanae*)

a mountain cherry tree
so eager to shed its blossoms
and efface itself

cherry blossoms, cherry
blossoms—at each and every stop
cherry blossoms

yamazakura hitasura chitte onore kesu (Tsuda, *Nanae*)

sakura sakura kakueki teisha shite sakura (Uda and Kuroda, *Joryū haiku shūsei*)

by the moonlit ocean
bereft of song
a bird and I

of this world
or the world beyond? on the sea
the sunset glow

TSUDA KIYOKO

tsukiyo no umi uta wo wasureta tori to ware (Uda and Kuroda, *Joryū haiku shūsei*)

ano yo to mo kono yo to mo umi yūyakete (*Haiku*, September 1996)

Inahata Teiko
b. 1931

"To sing of flowers and birds and copy things objectively is the way of traditional haiku. I have assiduously tried not to stray from that path."[1] Inahata Teiko wrote these words in her third book of haiku; she might have said she was following what Takahama Kyoshi taught. Teiko, a granddaughter of Kyoshi, has never wavered in her devotion to his legacy. In 2000 she opened the Kyoshi Memorial Museum near her home in Ashiya, a suburb of Kobe.

Teiko was born in Yokohama on 8 January 1931. Her father, Takahama Toshio (1900–1979), was Kyoshi's eldest son and successor as editor of *Hototogisu* (The mountain cuckoo). Teiko began writing haiku when she was small, as every child in her family did. As a student at Kobayashi Women's School of the Sacred Heart, she was converted to Roman Catholicism. Married in 1956, she has two sons and a daughter. Her haiku, which long remained unpublished, were finally collected in *Teiko kushū* (The collected haiku of Teiko) in 1976. After her father died in 1979, she became editor of *Hototogisu*. Her husband fell ill and died the following year. She gradually recovered from these deaths, and in 1985 she published *Teiko daini kushū* (The second collected haiku of Teiko). Two years later she organized the Japan Association for Traditional Haiku, of which she became the director. From around this time she

---

[1] Postscript to *Teiko daisan kushū*. Cited in Inahata, *Teihon Teiko kushū*, 214.

began to travel widely, making trips to Europe, North America, and China. Besides her other collections, *Teiko daisan kushū* (The third collected haiku of Teiko, 1990), *Shōji akari* (Light through the screens, 1996), and *Sayuragi* (Gentle swaying, 2001), Teiko has introduced many Japanese to haiku with such books as *Shizen to katariau yasashii haiku* (Easy haiku that talk with nature, 1978) and *Haiku ni shitashimu* (Growing familiar with haiku, 1985).

as if happiness
were waiting, the New
Year's calendar

a snowy mountain
and a mountain without snow
look about the same height

shiawase no machi iru gotoku hatsugoyomi (Inahata, *Teiko kushū*)

yukiyama mo yuki naki yama mo nishi takasa (Ibid.)

light breeze
but just enough to carry
plum blossoms' scent

rain in the field
arrives without sound—
a summer thistle

kaze sukoshi ari ume no ka wo hakobu hodo (Inahata, *Teiko daini kushū*)

no no ame wa oto naku itaru natsu azami (Ibid.)

side by side
one child drawing maple leaves
the other an elephant

losing my way
is part of the journey—
poppy flowers

momiji kaku ko ni zō wo kaku ko ga narabi (Inahata, *Teiko daini kushū*)

michi mayou koto mo tabiji yo keshi no hana (Ibid.)

the dead grass—
life lies dormant
on the face of the earth

                          flower buds
                          late to bloom, yet somehow
                          beginning to brim

kusa karete inochi hisomeshi chi no mo ari (Inahata, *Teiko daini kushū*)

hana okure iru mo minagiru mono no ari (Inahata, *Teiko daisan kushū*)

scent of magnolias
blocked now and then
by mountain air

butterflies, white
and yellow, on this day
of indecision

hō no ka wo toki ni saegiru sanki ari (Inahata, *Teiko daisan kushū*)

chō no shiro chō no ki kokoro mayou hi ni (Ibid.)

the tree peony
keeps color sealed
within its buds

icefish—
their lives transparent
in the rippling water

bōtan no iro wo akasanu tsubomi kana (Inahata, *Teiko daisan kushū*)

shirauo no inochi no sukete mizu ugoku (Ibid.)

standing stalk—
rugged and robust
at the end of life

nothing but a prayer
on this day when blossoms
beautifully fall

kuki tatsu ya inochi no hate wo takumashiku (Inahata, *Shōji akari*)

tada inoru rakka utsukushikarishi hi ni (Ibid.)

potato flowers
up and down, up and down
to the far horizon

in the Zen temple
stillness at high noon—
an ant lion's pit

INAHATA TEIKO

jagaimo no hana no kifuku no chiheisen (Inahata, *Shōji akari*)

zendera no hiru no shizukesa arijigoku (Ibid.)

while I'm being watched
it's hard to spit out
watermelon seeds

the instant it flies up
a dragonfly
loses its shadow

INAHATA TEIKO

mirare ite tane dashinikuki suika kana (Inahata, *Shōji akari*)

tobi tachite kage ushinaishi tonbo kana (Ibid.)

murmur of waves
unheeded by today's
wild daffodils

fireworks vanish
leaving the darkness
changed from before

INAHATA TEIKO

namioto no kyō wa todokazu nozuisen (Inahata, *Shōji akari*)

hanabi kie moto no yami de wa naku narishi (Hirai, *Gendai no haiku*)

Uda Kiyoko
b. 1935

autumn wind—   *akikaze ya*
with different patterns   *moyō no chigau*
two plates   *sara futatsu*

Uda Kiyoko, when still a beginner in haiku, asked at a haiku meeting why the first line of Hara Sekitei's (1886–1951) famous haiku should be "autumn wind" rather than, say, "spring wind." An older haiku poet replied that if the haiku had begun with "spring wind," the plates would have had the same pattern. The answer was convincing to Kiyoko, though she did not know how to explain it. The older poet was just an ordinary citizen, but he knew his haiku.[1] Since then, she has learned much from similar comments by a number of such people.

Born in Yamaguchi Prefecture on 15 October 1935, Uda Kiyoko graduated from Mukogawa Gakuin University near Kobe. Her introduction to haiku came in high school under the guidance of a haiku master named Tōyama Bakurō. But when she read Katsura Nobuko, she was immediately attracted to her haiku, and Nobuko's magazine, *Sōen* (The grass garden), became Kiyoko's preferred reading. Soon she brought out her first and second books of haiku, *Rira no ki* (Lilacs) in 1980 and *Natsu no hi* (Summer days) in 1983. The Modern Haiku Association Prize was awarded to her in 1982. Her poetic interests have been diverse: Maeda Masaharu (b. 1913), Kaneko

---

[1] Sōda, ed., *Gendai haiku shūsei*, 207.

Tōta, Takayanagi Shigenobu (1923–1983), Nakagami Kenji, Tsubouchi Toshinori (b. 1944), and others have all engaged her attention one way or another. She is also an outstanding critic of haiku, especially women's haiku. In 1999 she and Kuroda Momoko collected more than twelve thousand haiku by eighty-one women in *Joryū haiku shūsei* (The collection of women's haiku). Her sixth and most recent collection of haiku, published in 2000, is *Zō* (The elephant); it includes a lament for Nakagami's death[2] and reactions to the Kobe earthquake of 1995. She continues to edit *Sōen*.

---

[2] Nakagami Kenji died in 1992. Kiyoko respected him as a novelist who vigourously fought discrimination against social outcasts. Nakagami created Kumano as a mystic region that metaphorically and actually featured these outcasts.

so lonesome
when I write my name—
summer dawn

pond smelt
both in life and death
have their bodies bent

waga na kaku toki sabishiki yo natsu no ake (Uda, *Rira no ki*)

wakasagi wa seishi dochira mo dō wo mage (Ibid.)

saffron in bloom —
the movie yesterday
murdered a man

a scrap of iron —
without fail, menfolk
stop to look

UDA KIYOKO

safuran ya eiga wa kinō hito wo ayame (Uda, *Rira no ki*)

teppen ya kanarazu otoko ga tachidomaru (Uda, *Natsu no hi*)

the soul, the breasts
and all else are held in the arms
when autumn arrives

beautifully
the cremation ends
before noon

tamashii mo chibusa mo aki wa ude no naka (Uda, *Natsu no hi*)

utsukushiku kasō no owaru gozen kana (Ibid.)

dead firefly—
the entire night sky
beautifully clear

the moon in heaven—
on the earth, a hackneyed
tale of its wanderings

shinibotaru yo wa utsukushiku hare watari (Uda, *Natsu no hi*)

ten ni tsuki chi ni arifureta ryūridan (Uda, *Hantō*)

>   where the entire
>   mountain has been trampled
>   a lady flower

still alive
a dragonfly drying up
on a rock

UDA KIYOKO

yama hitotsu tsubushita ato no ominaeshi (Uda, *Hantō*)

ikinagara tonbō kawaku ishi no ue (Ibid.)

shrikes, trees, stones
all are in white —
time to start a trip?

                              half of the body
                              in a dream; the other half
                              in the snow

mozu mo ki mo ishi mo hakushoku tabi ni deru ka (Uda, *Hantō*)

hanshin wa yume hanshin wa yuki no naka (Ibid.)

faces with no mask
turn into masked faces
around the fire

neither white
nor yellow, chrysanthemums
in total darkness

UDA KIYOKO

hitamen mo kamen ni onaji hi no mawari (Uda, *Hantō*)

shiro mo ki mo arazu kikka no mayami naru (Uda, *Kagetsu shū*)

a swan
not so spotlessly white
as in a photo

        the blossom season
        comes to town, before the smell
        of fish is gone

shashin hodo hakuchō mashiro ni wa arazu (Uda, *Kagetsu shū*)

hanadoki no machi ni gyoshū no nukenu mama (Ibid.)

dangling wisteria—
how could aging be
this beautiful?

on the leaves
or under, every snail
has a will of its own

kakari fuji toshiyori kaku mo utsukushi ya (Uda, *Kagetsu shū*)

ha no omote ha no ura dendenmushi no ishi (*Haiku*, September 1995)

mountain leeches too
have something to say—
let's listen

                              beyond death
                              there's a future, hence we die—
                              here's crepe myrtle

yamahiru no iibun mo kikō de wa nai ka (Haiku, September 1997)

shi ni mirai areba koso shinu sarusuberi (Haiku, September 1998)

Kuroda Momoko
b. 1938

"Compose many haiku and throw away many" is Kuroda Momoko's advice to beginners. "In the process, you will discover the true state of your mind. If you start writing haiku, compose a lot of them"—as many as five a day.[1] Make your first haiku the starting point for the others. Then you can be the first to choose which one comes closest to what you want to express. The rest can be thrown away without reluctance.

This attitude partly reflects Kuroda Momoko's busy career. Born in Tokyo on 10 August 1938, she was evacuated in middle school to northern Tochigi Prefecture, where her mother took her to a *kukai*, or haiku meeting. Later, as a psychology major at Tokyo Women's University, she regularly took part in a haiku group led by Yamaguchi Seison (1892–1988). Yet when she graduated, she went to work for Hakuhōdō, a public relations company, and wrote no haiku for the next ten years. Then, confined to a hospital bed by an accident, she came across an encyclopedia of season words. Reawakened to haiku, she began attending Seison's *kukai* again. In 1982 her first book of haiku, *Ki no isu* (The wooden chair), won the Women's Prize in Modern Haiku and the Haiku Association New Poet's Prize. She started the magazine *Aoi* (Growing up) in 1990. Two years later her third collection, *Ichimoku issō* (Every tree and grass), was awarded the Haiku Association Prize. She has made a number of "pilgrimages" or haiku journeys to

---

[1] Kuroda, *Kyō kara hajimeru haiku*, 132.

famous places: the Cherry Blossom Pilgrimage through Japan took her twenty-eight years to complete, and the Pilgrimage to Hiroshige's One Hundred Views of Edo took her nine years. In 1998 she retired from her public relations job to concentrate on haiku. She has also published several books of practical advice for haiku poets—for instance, *Anata no haiku-zukuri* (Your haiku composition) in 1987, *Kyō kara hajimeru haiku* (Haiku begins today) in 1992, and *Kuroda Momoko saijiki* (Kuroda Momoko's book of season words) in 1998.

a lightning flash
soaked in green glaze
far beyond the field

white leek
turned into light beam
now being cut up

KURODA MOMOKO

inazuma no ryokushū wo abu no no hate ni (Kuroda, *Ki no isu*)

shironegi no hikari no bō wo ima kizamu (Ibid.)

each fresh day
inflicting new wounds
on a white peony

nightshades in bloom—
as if in the depth of water
this island's darkness

KURODA MOMOKO

atarashiki hi ni itami yuku hakubotan (Kuroda, *Ki no isu*)

dachura saku suitei ni nite shima no yami (Ibid.)

the sound of waves—
drawing near, I become part
of the winter scene

cooking trout—
in the solitary house
a smell of night

KURODA MOMOKO

namioto ni chikazuku ware mo fuyugeshiki (Kuroda, *Mizu no tobira*)

ayu wo nite yoru no nioi no ikken'ya (Ibid.)

this bluffer's diary
has no more space for me
to write in

they pass each other—
a dog, a man, and a sleigh
carrying a coffin

tsuyogari no nikki haten to shite itari (Kuroda, *Mizu no tobira*)

surechigau inu to otoko to hitsugizori (Ibid.)

on my palm
a blue firefly
smelling of water

light through the leaves—
gigantic all of a sudden
a mountain ant

te no naka ni mizu no nioi no aobotaru (Kuroda, *Mizu no tobira*)

komorebi ya niwaka ni ōki yama no ari (Ibid.)

on each bridge
the voice of darkness
the cry of insects

fugu soup—
on the wall, a great big
John Lennon

hashi wataru tabi yami no koe mushi no koe (Kuroda, *Mizu no tobira*)

fugunabe ya kabe ni ōkina Jon Renon (Ibid.)

while the one
peels a white peach
the other weeps

immersing itself
in the Ganges River
the New Year's sun

KURODA MOMOKO

shiromomo wo hitori ga mukite hitori naku (Kuroda, *Ichimoku issō*)

ganjisu ni mi wo shizumetaru hatsuhi kana (Ibid.)

those thunderclouds—
in my neighbor's yard
a white peony

on a youngster's
open umbrella
spring snow

raiun ya tonari no niwa no hakubotan (Kuroda, Ichimoku issō)

kasa hirakitaru seinen ni haru no yuki (Ibid.)

whispering
something to the rose
she cuts the rose

peony so white —
on its leaves too,
ice-pure raindrops

KURODA MOMOKO

nanigoto ka bara ni tsubuyaki bara wo kiru (Kuroda, *Ichimoku issō*)

hakubotan ha ni mo kōri no yōna ame (*Haiku*, July 1994)

black swallowtails
in the grove, each
with a different crest

cloudy sky—
the peony's radiance
brimming over

kuroageha rinchū ni mon mina chigau (Haiku, September 1994)

donten ya botan no hikari koso afure (Haiku, July 1995)

Tsuji Momoko
b. 1945

Walking one day in winter, Tsuji Momoko noticed a house with a rattan blind. Why a sun blind in winter? She looked at it—then realized someone in the house was looking at her. All of a sudden a haiku came to her:

someone looks at me	*kochira miru*
from beyond a rattan blind	*fuyu no sudare no*
on a winter day	*mukō yori*[1]

This episode, from the beginning of one of her books, shows how easy it is to create a haiku. And that is characteristic of her: she uses haiku for recording the moment even as it disappears.

Tsuji Momoko, whose family name is Shimizu, was born in Yokohama on 4 February 1945. Educated at Waseda University, she first took up free verse but gradually began to concentrate on haiku. Kusumoto Kenkichi (1922–1988), Takayanagi Shigenobu, and Hatano Sōha (1923–1991) helped her in one way or another, as did her mother in her earlier years. She sent her haiku to *Taka* (The hawk) and got advice from its editor, Fujita Shōshi (b. 1926). Her haiku collections include *Momo* (Peaches, 1984), *Hirugao* (Bindweed flowers, 1987), *Dōji* (Children, 1991), *Nemu* (Silk trees, 1994), *Enokoro* (Puppies, 1997), and several others. She has also written books of advice for

---

[1] Tsuji, *Haiku no tsukurikata*, 9.

haiku poets, including *Haiku no tsukurikata* (How to write haiku, 1988), *Haiku saijiki* (Haiku book of season words, 1998), and *Momoko no irohani haiku* (Momoko's ABC of haiku, 1999). The magazine *Dōji* (Children), which she started in 1987, now has some five hundred regular subscribers. She is also skilled in *haiga* and operates a school that teaches it.

holding a knife
I feast my eyes
on a rain shower

still on my body
a tire tube for floating
I've bought at the store

hōchō wo motte shūu ni mitoretaru (Tsuji, *Momo*)

dōtai ni hamete ukiwa wo katte kuru (Ibid.)

autumn wind—
a saucepan of curry
is downed at once

at the uptown platform
and at the downtown platform too
new graduates

TSUJI MOMOKO

akikaze ya karē hitonabe sugu ni kara (Tsuji, *Hirugao*)

nobori hōmu kudari hōmu ni sotsugyōshi (Tsuji, *Dōji*)

about you
it knows nothing—
a spring crab

with a man
at Kentucky Fried Chicken
I grieve spring's departure

kimi no koto nan ni mo shirazu haru no kani (Tsuji, *Dōji*)

Kentakkii no ojisan to haru oshimikeri (Ibid.)

one who loves someone
with the one who doesn't
drinks beer

mid-autumn days—
a silver bracelet
strangling my arm

TSUJI MOMOKO

koi seshi hito koi naki hito to biiru kumu (Tsuji, *Dōji*)

chūshū ya gin no udewa ga ude shimete (Ibid.)

looks like the rough sea
on the sweet potato field—
a storm rages

for hanging a mask
and hanging sunglasses
ears in spring[1]

---

[1] In order not to spread infection, the Japanese often wear surgical masks when they have a cold.

araumi no yōnaru imo no arashi kana (Tsuji, *Dōji*)

masuku kake sangurasu kake haru no mimi (Ibid.)

green caterpillars—
one is crushed, while the other
still moves

                                in this shop
                                if you sit at this spot
                                a draught of air

TSUJI MOMOKO

imomushi no hitotsu wa tsubure hitotsu ayumu (Tsuji, *Nemu*)

kono mise no koko ni suwareba sukimakaze (Ibid.)

here comes a dog
seeing off the car
on a mountain trolley

here's the fish basket —
bindweed flowers
buried underneath

inu ga kite tozan ressha wo miokureru (Tsuji, *Nemu*)

biku oite hirugao no hana shitajiki ni (Tsuji, *Enokoro*)

to a drone fly
the pumpkin flower's inside
is snug

until they melt
hailstones retain
their original shape

TSUJI MOMOKO

hanaabu ni kabocha no hana no naka nukuki (Tsuji, *Enokoro*)

tokeru made arare no katachi shite orinu (Ibid.)

every one of them
in mourning clothes
under a parasol

into plain rubbish
they begin to turn—
fallen blossoms

TSUJI MOMOKO

zen'in ga mofuku de higasa sashite ori (Tsuji, *Enokoro*)

tada no gomi ni nari kakete iru hana no chiri (Sōda, *Gendai haiku shūsei*)

the butterfly—
its face is the same
as a caterpillar's

exhausted
they fan each other—
dancing girls

TSUJI MOMOKO

chōchō no kemushi no kao wo itashikeri (Sōda, Gendai haiku shūsei)

kutaburete augi au nari odori no ko (Uda and Kuroda, Joryū haiku shūsei)

Katayama Yumiko
b. 1952

"Not many young people think of haiku as a means of self-expression. Yet some of my contemporaries always choose it for themselves. I feel haiku may quietly live on with these people." Such is the conclusion of Katayama Yumiko in her article, "Josei haiku no mirai" (The future of women's haiku). She has no excessive expectations of haiku, but she does not minimize its value, either. "By looking at things that are not noticed except by haiku poets," she says, "women may feel a bit happier and better to be alive. I want haiku to give them this opportunity."[1]

Born on the seacoast in Chiba Prefecture on 17 July 1952, Katayama Yumiko first wanted to be a pianist and graduated in piano at Ueno Gakuen College. She was especially fond of Johannes Brahms. Among the households where she gave piano lessons was that of a couple whose hobby was haiku. She was introduced to their teacher Takaha Shugyō (b. 1930) and his magazine *Kari* (Hunting) in 1980. She began writing haiku, which at some point became her main activity. She has published four volumes of haiku: *Ame no uta* (Songs of rain, 1984), *Suisei* (The water sprite, 1989), *Tenkyū* (The celestial bow, 1995), and *Katayama Yumiko kushū* (The collected haiku of Katayama Yumiko, 1999). She is also an excellent haiku critic who has written such books as *Gendai*

---

[1] Katayama, "Josei haiku no mirai," in *Shinseiki joryū haiku wandārando*, ed. Katayama and Itami, 9–10.

haiku joryū hyakunin (One hundred women poets in contemporary haiku) in 1993 and *Gendai haiku to no taiwa* (Dialogues with contemporary haiku) in 1994. The latter won the New Critic's Award of the Association of Haiku Poets in 1994, while a revised (and definitive) edition of the former was reissued by another publisher in 1999.

the sound of waves
reaching my toe tips, I recline
in this rattan chair

departure bells
have lingered a while—
hazy spring sky

tsumasaki ni todoku shiosai tō neisu (Katayama, *Ame no uta*)

hassha beru ni mo aru yoin hanagumori (Ibid.)

floating weeds
continue to drift to one side
as night falls

prolonged
aftermath of a falling stone—
the mountain sleeps

KATAYAMA YUMIKO

ukikusa no katayorishi mama yo to nareri (Katayama, *Ame no uta*)

rakuseki no yoin wo nagaku yama nemuru (Ibid.)

hung on the wall
it turns into a flower—
a summer hat

though far from depressed
my face is buried
under a muffler

kabe ni kakereba hana to nari natsu bōshi (Katayama, Suisei)

sabishikaranedo mafurā ni kao uzume (Ibid.)

a lotus leaf
lets something radiant
spill out of itself

                                        postblossom foliage —
                                        differently white
                                        salt and sugar

hasu no ha no mabushiki mono wo koboshikeri (Katayama, *Suisei*)

hazakura ya shirosa chigaete shio satō (Ibid.)

someone's voice —
the morning glories
begin to fade

with a pencil
I torture an ant
on the desk at night

hitogoe no shite asagao no nae hajimu (Katayama, Suisei)

enpitsu de ari wo sainamu yo no kijō (Ibid.)

swept away
no larger than a flower petal
floating ice

                                  all the bulbs
                                  look somehow crooked—
                                  I plant them in the yard

nagasarete hanabira hodo no ukigōri (Katayama, *Suisei*)

mina doko ka yugamu kyūkon uenikeri (Ibid.)

no poem to poverty
in this age of ours—
an eggplant flower[1]

a child playing
with water in the garden
all alone

---

[1] Common people in Japan used to raise eggplants, cucumbers, and turnips in their vegetable gardens to supplement their meals.

mazushisa no shi to wa naranu yo nasu no hana (Katayama, *Suisei*)

mizu asobi suru ko ga niwa ni hitori kiri (Ibid.)

from the branch
that touches the blue sky
plum blossoms open

nesting swallows
haven't seen my sullen face —
or have they?

aozora ni fureshi eda yori ume hiraku (Uda and Kuroda, *Joryū haiku shūsei*)

sutsubame ni fukigenna kao mirareshi ya (Ibid.)

       falling
       like broken promises
       spring snow

cherry blossoms
in full bloom, and above them
the sky

yakusoku wo tagaeshi gotoku haru no yuki (Uda and Kuroda, *Joryū haiku shūsei*)

mankai no sakura no ue ni sora no ari (Ibid.)

beyond the skylight
constellations go—
last year, this year

in the spider's web
nothing is caught
at high noon

KATAYAMA YUMIKO

tenmado wo sugi yuku seiza kozo kotoshi (Uda and Kuroda, *Joryū haiku shūsei*)

kumo no i ni kakaru mono naki mahiru kana (Ibid.)

Mayuzumi Madoka
b. 1965

"For me, composing haiku means 'gathering treasures,'" says Mayuzumi Madoka. "The moment I feel is more clearly printed in my heart than on any beautiful picture postcard."[1] The moments she speaks of include many things that come from the West—a Porsche, a McDonald's hamburger, a polo shirt, a German shepherd, sunglasses. Madoka is a modern woman who lives in a large city and is familiar with all these things. She is smart, sophisticated, and contemporary.

Madoka's father is Mayuzumi Shū (b. 1930), a haiku poet who edits the magazine *Haruno* (The spring field). Born in Kanagawa Prefecture on 31 July 1965, she was educated at Ferris Women's College and was later selected as Miss Kimono. She became seriously interested in haiku when working as a television reporter on a segment on the poet Sugita Hisajo. Her first collection, *B-men no natsu* (Summer on the B-side), earned her the Kadokawa Haiku Encouragement Award in 1994. Two years later she founded *Gekkan Heppubān* (Monthly Hepburn), a haiku magazine for women who aspire to living as freely as Audrey Hepburn did in her movie roles. It now has some five hundred regular subscribers grouped in Tokyo, Osaka, Nagoya, and several other places. Madoka has since published the long haiku essay *Seiya no asa* (The morning after the Christmas eve, 1996), the haiku books *Hanagoromo* (Clothes for flower viewing, 1997) and *Kuchizuke* (The

---

[1] *Haiku*, June 1994, 133.

kiss, 1999), the bilingual haiku collection *Love in Kyoto* (2001), and edited the volume *Heppbān na onnatachi* (Hepburn-like Women, 2000), among other projects. She has proposed some new season words, such as "whale watching" (summer), "herb tea" (autumn), and "cocoa" (winter). In 1998 she went to China and lectured at Beijing Foreign Language University and Tenshin Nanhai University. In 2000 she gave a talk in Chicago.

Mother's Day—
I end up making
my mother cry

we gather herbs
after arriving
in a red Porsche

MAYUZUMI MADOKA

haha no hi no haha wo nakashite shimaikeri (Mayuzumi, B-men no natsu)

yomogi tsumu akai Porushe de noritsukete (Ibid.)

mannequins
whispering among themselves—
hazy spring night

                              choosing a swimsuit—
                              when did his eyes
                              replace mine?

manekin no sasayaki aeru oboro kana (Mayuzumi, *B-men no natsu*)

mizugi erabu itsu shika kare no me to natte (Ibid.)

like a dead
body, I try to stay afloat
in the pool

impelled to dream
of soaring in the sky—
goldfish at night

shinda mane shite uite miru pūru kana (Mayuzumi, *B-men no natsu*)

tobu yume wo mitakute yoru no kingyo-tachi (Ibid.)

after letting it
swing a while, I pop the cherry
into my mouth

more than a brother
less than a lover
behind shaved ice[1]

[1] In Japan, a dish of shaved ice is a popular refreshment in summer.

shibaraku wa yurashite fukumu sakuranbo (Mayuzumi, *B-men no natsu*)

ani ijō koibito miman kakigōri (Ibid.)

among the fountains
a leading actor
and those in support

now the trip is over—
my summer holidays
start their B-side

funsui ni shuyaku wakiyaku arinikeri (Mayuzumi, *B-men no natsu*)

tabi oete yori B-men no natsuyasumi (Ibid.)

with a look
of unconcern, the full moon
hanging above you

                              the circus gone—
                              it has become a town
                              of autumn wind

shiranpuri shite mangetsu ga kimi no ue (Mayuzumi, B-men no natsu)

sākasu ga hane akikaze no machi to naru (Ibid.)

with neither an entrance
nor an exit, the huge
field-crop of flowers

emerging from the rubbish
swept into a pile
winter's bee

iriguchi mo deguchi mo nakute ōhanano (Mayuzumi, *B-men no natsu*)

haki yoseshi chiri no naka yori fuyu no hachi (Ibid.)

Tokyo
not a thing stirring—
the year's first scene

                                        in my New Year's dream
                                        no pumpkin carriage
                                        makes its appearance

Tōkyō ga jitto shite iru hatsugeshiki (Mayuzumi, *B-men no natsu*)

hatsuyume ni kabocha no basha no arawarezu (Ibid.)

pretending
not to have heard, I sip
a soda drink

a shooting star—
in love with someone, not knowing
where it will lead me

kikoenai furi wo shite sū sōdasui (Haiku, September 1994)

ryūsei ya yukue shirazu no koi wo shite (Mayuzumi, *Seiya no asa*)

winter waves
so blue they keep people
at a distance

                                                        watermelon
                                                        is served, ending the quarrel
                                                        between brothers

fuyunami no hito tōzakeru aosa kana (Mayuzumi, *Hanagaromo*)

suika dete kyōdai genka owarikeri (*Haiku*, January 1999)

Selected Bibliography

Works in English

Blyth, R. H. *Haiku*. 4 vols. Tokyo: Hokuseido, 1949–52.
———. *A History of Haiku*. 2 vols. Tokyo: Hokuseido, 1963–64.
Donegan, Patricia, and Yoshie Ishibashi. *Chiyoni: Woman Haiku Master*. Tokyo: Tuttle, 1998.
Henderson, Harold G. *An Introduction to Haiku*. Garden City, N.Y.: Doubleday, 1958.
Higginson, William J. *The Haiku Handbook*. New York: McGraw-Hill, 1985.
Katō, Kōko, and David Burleigh, trans. *A Hidden Pond: Anthology of Modern Haiku*. Tokyo: Kadokawa Shoten, 1997.
Keene, Donald. *Dawn to the West*. 2 vols. New York: Holt, Rinehart & Winston, 1984.
———. *World Within Walls*. New York: Holt, Rinehart & Winston, 1976.
Maeda, Cana, trans. *Monkey's Raincoat*. New York: Grossman, 1973.
Mayuzumi, Madoka. *Love in Kyoto*. Kyoto: PHP Interface, 2001.
Miner, Earl, and Hiroko Odagiri, trans. *The Monkey's Straw Raincoat and Other Poetry of the Bashō School*. Princeton: Princeton University Press, 1981.
Sato, Hiroaki, and Burton Watson, eds. *From the Country of Eight Islands*. Garden City, N.Y.: Anchor/Doubleday, 1981.
Shiffert, Edith Marcomb, and Yūki Sawa, eds. *Anthology of Modern Japanese Poetry*. Tokyo: Tuttle, 1972.
Suzuki, Masajo. *Love Haiku: Masajo Suzuki's Lifetime of Love*. Trans. Lee Gurga and Emiko Miyashita. Decatur, Ill.: Brooks Books, 2000.
Yasuda, Kenneth. *The Japanese Haiku*. Tokyo: Tuttle, 1957.
Yoshino, Yoshiko. *Budding Sakura*. Trans. Jack Stamm. Evanston, Ill.: Deep North Press, 2000.
———. *Tsuru*. Trans. Lee Gurga and Emiko Miyashita. Evanston, Ill.: Deep North Press, 2001.

Works in Japanese

All publishers below are located in Tokyo unless noted otherwise.

Akimoto, Matsuyo. *Yama hototogisu hoshii mama*. N.p., 1966.
Asō, Isoji, et al., eds. *Haiku taikan*. Meiji Shoin, 1971.
Bessho, Makiko. *Bashō ni hirakareta haikai no joseishi*. Orijin Shuppan Sentā, 1989.
Ebara, Taizō. *Haiku hyōshaku*. 2 vols. Kadokawa Shoten, 1953.
Ebara, Taizō, et al., eds. *Teihon Saikaku zenshū*. 14 vols. Chūō Kōron Sha, 1949–75.
Furuya, Tomoyoshi, ed. *Edo jidai joryū bungaku zenshū*. 4 vols. Nihon Tosho Sentā, 1979.
Gendai joryū haiku zenshū. 6 vols. Kōdansha, 1980–81.
Haiku. Kadokawa Shoten, 1952–.
Haiku kōza. 10 vols. Kaizōsha, 1932.
Hashimoto, Takako. *Hashimoto Takako zen kushū*. Rippū Shobō, 1973.
Hirai, Shōbin, ed. *Gendai no haiku*. Kōdansha, 1993.
Hisamatsu, Sen'ichi, and Imoto Nōichi, eds. *Koten haibungaku taikei*. 16 vols. Shūeisha, 1970–72.
Horikiri, Minoru. *Shōmon meika kusen*. 2 vols. Iwanami Shoten, 1989.
Iida, Ryūta, et al., eds. *Kanshō gendai haiku zenshū*. 12 vols. Rippū Shobō, 1980–81.
Inahata, Teiko. *Sayuragi*. Asahi Shinbun Sha, 2001.
———. *Shōji akari*. Kadokawa Shoten, 1996.
———. *Teihon Teiko kushū*. Kadokawa Shoten, 1998.
———. *Teiko daini kushū*. Nagata Shobō, 1985.
———. *Teiko daisan kushū*. Nagata Shobō, 1990.
———. *Teiko kushū*. Shinjusha, 1976.
Ishibashi, Hideno. *Sakura koku*. Sōgensha, 1949.
Jambor, Kinuko. *Haikaishi Sonome no shōgai*. Nagata Shobō, 2000.
Katayama, Yumiko. *Ame no uta*. Hon'ami Shoten, 1984.
———. *Gendai haiku joryū hyakunin*. Bokuyōsha, 1993. Republished as *Teihon gendai haiku joryū hyakunin*. Hokumeisha, 1999.
———. *Gendai haiku to no taiwa*. Hon'ami Shoten, 1994.
———. *Katayama Yumiko kushū*. Sunagoya Shobō, 1998.
———. *Suisei*. Hon'ami Shoten, 1989.
———. *Tenkyū*. Kadokawa Shoten, 1995.
Katayama, Yumiko, and Itami Keiko, eds. *Shinseiki joryū haiku wandārando*. Chūsekisha, 1999.

Katsumine, Shinpū, ed. *Keishū haika zenshū*. Shūeikaku, 1922.
——, ed. *Nihon haisho taikei*. 15 vols. Nihon Haisho Taikei Kankōkai, 1925–30.
Katsura, Nobuko. *Banshun*. Azabu Shobō, 1967.
——. *Gekkō shō*. Seiunsha, 1949.
——. *Juei*. Rippū Shobō, 1991.
——. *Kaei*. Rippū Shobō, 1996.
——. *Nyoshin*. Rōkandō, 1955.
——. *Shinryoku*. Bokuyōsha, 1974.
Kawashima, Tsuyu. *Joryū haijin*. Meiji Shoin, 1957.
Kawata, Jun, ed. *Kikushani hokku zenshū*. Sara Shoten, 1937.
Kokugo kokubun. Kyoto: Kyoto Daigaku Kokubun Gakkai. 1931–.
Kuriyama, Riichi, et al., eds. *Kinsei haiku haibunshū*. Vol. 42, *Nihon koten bungaku zenshū*. Shōgakukan, 1972.
Kuroda, Momoko. *Ichimoku issō*. Kashinsha, 1992.
——. *Ki no isu*. Bokuyōsha, 1981.
——. *Kyō kara hajimeru haiku*. Shōgakukan, 1992.
——. *Mizu no tobira*. Bokuyōsha, 1983.
Matsumoto, Seichō. "Kiku makura." *Bungei shunjū* (August 1953).
Mayuzumi, Madoka. *B-men no natsu*. Kadokawa Shoten, 1994.
——. *Hanagoromo*. PHP Kenkyūjo, 1997
——. *Kuchizuke*. Kadokawa Haruki Jimusho, 1999.
——. *Seiya no asa*. Asahi Shinbun Sha, 1996.
Mitsuhashi, Takajo. *Mitsuhashi Takajo zen kushū*. Rippū Shobō, 1976.
Mori, Shigeo. *Den Sutejo*. Seiunsha, 1928.
Nakamoto, Jodō, ed. *Kaga no Chiyo zenshū*. Kanazawa: Kaga no Chiyo Zenshū Kankōkai, 1955.
Nakamura, Sonoko, et al., eds. *Gendai shiika shū* Vol. 24, *Josei sakka shiriizu*. Kadokawa Shoten, 1999.
Nishitani, Seinosuke. *Tenmei haijin ron*. Kōransha, 1929.
Ogata, Tsutomu, et al., eds. *Buson zenshū*. 9 vols. Kōdansha, 1992–.
Ōno, Rinka, et al., eds. *Kindai haiku taikan*. Meiji Shoin, 1974.
Saitō, Shinji, et al., eds. *Gendai haiku handobukku*. Yūzankaku, 1995.
Sekimori, Katsuo. *Ōmi shōmon haiku no kanshō*. Tōkyōdō, 1993.
Sōda, Yasumasa, ed. *Gendai haiku shūsei*. Rippū Shobō, 1996.
Sugita, Hisajo. *Sugita Hisajo kushū*. Kadokawa Shoten, 1952.
Takeshita, Shizunojo. *Takeshita Shizunojo kubunshū*. Hoshi Shobō, 1964.
Tomiyasu, Fūsei, et al., eds. *Gendai haiku taikei*. 12 vols. Kadokawa Shoten, 1980–81.
Tsuda, Kiyoko. *Jūsō*. Bokuyōsha, 1982.

———. *Kuzugoromo*. Nara: Kei no Kai, 1988.
———. *Muhō*. Henshū Kōbō IT, 2000.
———. *Nanae*. Henshū Kōbō Noa, 1991.
———. *Nininshō*. Bokuyōsha, 1973.
———. *Raihai*. Kondō Shoten, 1959.
Tsuji, Momoko. *Dōji*. Kadokawa Shoten, 1991.
———. *Enokoro*. Yū Shorin, 1997.
———. *Haiku no tsukurikata*. Seibidō Shuppan, 1988.
———. *Hirugao*. Gyararii Shiki, 1986.
———. *Momo*. Bokuyōsha, 1984.
———. *Nemu*. Chōfu: Furansudō, 1994.
———. *Tsuji Momoko kushū*. Chōfu: Furansudō, 1993.
Uda, Kiyoko. *Hantō*. Kumano Daigaku Shuppankyoku, 1992.
———. *Kagetsu shū*. N.p., 1995.
———. *Natsu no hi*. Osaka: Kaifūsha, 1983.
———. *Rira no ki*. Osaka: Sōen Hakkōsho, 1980.
———. *Uda Kiyoko kushū*. Chōfu: Furansudō, 1992.
———. *Zō*. Kadokawa Shoten, 2000.
Uda, Kiyoko, and Kuroda Momoko, eds. *Joryū haiku shūsei*. Rippū Shobō, 1999.
Ueno, Sachiko. *Josei haiku no sekai*. Iwanami Shoten, 1989.
———. *Kindai no joryū haiku*. Ōfūsha, 1978.
Yamamoto, Kenkichi. *Yamamoto Kenkichi haiku tokuhon*. 5 vols. Kadokawa Shoten, 1992.
Yamanaka, Rokuhiko. *Chiyojo to Kikushani*. Jinbun Shoin, 1942.
Yoshino, Yoshiko. *Hatsuarashi*. Chūō Kōkon Jigyō Shuppan, 1971.
———. *Kashin*. Kadokawa Shoten, 1984.
———. *Kurenai*. Rōkandō, 1956.
———. *Ryūsui*. Kadokawa Shoten, 2000.
———. *Yoshino Yoshiko shū*. Ser. 3, Vol. 54, *Jichū gendai haiku shiriizu*. Haijin Kyōkai, 1983.
Yoshiya, Nobuko. *Soko no nuketa hishaku*. Shinchōsha, 1964.
Zoku haiku kōza. 8 vols. Kaizōsha, 1934.

OTHER WORKS IN THE COLUMBIA ASIAN STUDIES SERIES

TRANSLATIONS FROM THE ASIAN CLASSICS

Major Plays of Chikamatsu, tr. Donald Keene	1961
Four Major Plays of Chikamatsu, tr. Donald Keene. Paperback ed. only.	1961; rev. ed. 1997
Records of the Grand Historian of China, translated from the Shih chi of Ssu-ma Ch'ien, tr. Burton Watson, 2 vols.	1961
Instructions for Practical Living and Other Neo-Confucian Writings by Wang Yang-ming, tr. Wing-tsit Chan	1963
Hsün Tzu: Basic Writings, tr. Burton Watson, paperback ed. only.	1963; rev. ed. 1996
Chuang Tzu: Basic Writings, tr. Burton Watson, paperback ed. only.	1964; rev. ed. 1996
The Mahābhārata, tr. Chakravarthi V. Narasimhan. Also in paperback ed.	1965; rev. ed. 1997
The Manyōshū, Nippon Gakujutsu Shinkōkai edition	1965
Su Tung-p'o: Selections from a Sung Dynasty Poet, tr. Burton Watson. Also in paperback ed.	1965
Bhartrihari: Poems, tr. Barbara Stoler Miller. Also in paperback ed.	1967
Basic Writings of Mo Tzu, Hsün Tzu, and Han Fei Tzu, tr. Burton Watson. Also in separate paperback eds.	1967
The Awakening of Faith, Attributed to Aśvaghosha, tr. Yoshito S. Hakeda. Also in paperback ed.	1967
Reflections on Things at Hand: The Neo-Confucian Anthology, comp. Chu Hsi and Lü Tsu-ch'ien, tr. Wing-tsit Chan	1967
The Platform Sutra of the Sixth Patriarch, tr. Philip B. Yampolsky. Also in paperback ed.	1967

Essays in Idleness: The Tsurezuregusa of Kenkō, tr. Donald Keene. Also in paperback ed. — 1967

The Pillow Book of Sei Shōnagon, tr. Ivan Morris, 2 vols. — 1967

Two Plays of Ancient India: The Little Clay Cart and the Minister's Seal, tr. J. A. B. van Buitenen — 1968

The Complete Works of Chuang Tzu, tr. Burton Watson — 1968

The Romance of the Western Chamber (Hsi Hsiang chi), tr. S. I. Hsiung. Also in paperback ed. — 1968

The Manyōshū, Nippon Gakujutsu Shinkōkai edition. Paperback ed. only. — 1969

Records of the Historian: Chapters from the Shih chi of Ssu-ma Ch'ien, tr. Burton Watson. Paperback ed. only. — 1969

Cold Mountain: 100 Poems by the T'ang Poet Han-shan, tr. Burton Watson. Also in paperback ed. — 1970

Twenty Plays of the Nō Theatre, ed. Donald Keene. Also in paperback ed. — 1970

Chūshingura: The Treasury of Loyal Retainers, tr. Donald Keene. Also in paperback ed. — 1971; rev. ed. 1997

The Zen Master Hakuin: Selected Writings, tr. Philip B. Yampolsky — 1971

Chinese Rhyme-Prose: Poems in the Fu Form from the Han and Six Dynasties Periods, tr. Burton Watson. Also in paperback ed. — 1971

Kūkai: Major Works, tr. Yoshito S. Hakeda. Also in paperback ed. — 1972

The Old Man Who Does as He Pleases: Selections from the Poetry and Prose of Lu Yu, tr. Burton Watson — 1973

The Lion's Roar of Queen Śrīmālā, tr. Alex and Hideko Wayman — 1974

Courtier and Commoner in Ancient China: Selections from the History of the Former Han by Pan Ku, tr. Burton Watson. Also in paperback ed. — 1974

Japanese Literature in Chinese, vol. 1: *Poetry and Prose in Chinese by Japanese Writers of the Early Period*, tr. Burton Watson — 1975

Japanese Literature in Chinese, vol. 2: *Poetry and Prose in Chinese by Japanese Writers of the Later Period*, tr. Burton Watson — 1976

Scripture of the Lotus Blossom of the Fine Dharma, tr. Leon Hurvitz. Also in paperback ed. — 1976

Love Song of the Dark Lord: Jayadeva's Gītagovinda,
tr. Barbara Stoler Miller. Also in paperback ed.
Cloth ed. includes critical text of the Sanskrit. 1977; rev. ed. 1997
Ryōkan: Zen Monk-Poet of Japan, tr. Burton Watson 1977
Calming the Mind and Discerning the Real: From the Lam rim chen mo of Tson-kha-pa, tr. Alex Wayman 1978
The Hermit and the Love-Thief: Sanskrit Poems of Bhartrihari and Bilhaṇa, tr. Barbara Stoler Miller 1978
The Lute: Kao Ming's P'i-p'a chi, tr. Jean Mulligan. Also in paperback ed. 1980
A Chronicle of Gods and Sovereigns: Jinnō Shōtōki of Kitabatake Chikafusa, tr. H. Paul Varley 1980
Among the Flowers: The Hua-chien chi, tr. Lois Fusek 1982
Grass Hill: Poems and Prose by the Japanese Monk Gensei, tr. Burton Watson 1983
Doctors, Diviners, and Magicians of Ancient China: Biographies of Fang-shih, tr. Kenneth J. DeWoskin. Also in paperback ed. 1983
Theater of Memory: The Plays of Kālidāsa, ed. Barbara Stoler Miller. Also in paperback ed. 1984
The Columbia Book of Chinese Poetry: From Early Times to the Thirteenth Century, ed. and tr. Burton Watson. Also in paperback ed. 1984
Poems of Love and War: From the Eight Anthologies and the Ten Long Poems of Classical Tamil, tr. A. K. Ramanujan. Also in paperback ed. 1985
The Bhagavad Gita: Krishna's Counsel in Time of War, tr. Barbara Stoler Miller 1986
The Columbia Book of Later Chinese Poetry, ed. and tr. Jonathan Chaves. Also in paperback ed. 1986
The Tso Chuan: Selections from China's Oldest Narrative History, tr. Burton Watson 1989
Waiting for the Wind: Thirty-six Poets of Japan's Late Medieval Age, tr. Steven Carter 1989
Selected Writings of Nichiren, ed. Philip B. Yampolsky 1990
Saigyō, Poems of a Mountain Home, tr. Burton Watson 1990
The Book of Lieh Tzu: A Classic of the Tao, tr. A. C. Graham. Morningside ed. 1990
The Tale of an Anklet: An Epic of South India—The Cilappatikāram of Iḷaṅkō Aṭikaḷ, tr. R. Parthasarathy 1993
Waiting for the Dawn: A Plan for the Prince, tr. and introduction by Wm. Theodore de Bary 1993
Yoshitsune and the Thousand Cherry Trees: A Masterpiece of the Eighteenth-Century Japanese Puppet

Theater, tr., annotated, and with introduction by Stanleigh H. Jones, Jr. — 1993

The Lotus Sutra, tr. Burton Watson. Also in paperback ed. — 1993

The Classic of Changes: A New Translation of the I Ching as Interpreted by Wang Bi, tr. Richard John Lynn — 1994

Beyond Spring: Tz'u Poems of the Sung Dynasty, tr. Julie Landau — 1994

The Columbia Anthology of Traditional Chinese Literature, ed. Victor H. Mair — 1994

Scenes for Mandarins: The Elite Theater of the Ming, tr. Cyril Birch — 1995

Letters of Nichiren, ed. Philip B. Yampolsky; tr. Burton Watson et al. — 1996

Unforgotten Dreams: Poems by the Zen Monk Shōtetsu, tr. Steven D. Carter — 1997

The Vimalakirti Sutra, tr. Burton Watson — 1997

Japanese and Chinese Poems to Sing: The Wakan rōei shū, tr. J. Thomas Rimer and Jonathan Chaves — 1997

A Tower for the Summer Heat, Li Yu, tr. Patrick Hanan — 1998

Traditional Japanese Theater: An Anthology of Plays, Karen Brazell — 1998

The Original Analects: Sayings of Confucius and His Successors (0479–0249), E. Bruce Brooks and A. Taeko Brooks — 1998

The Classic of the Way and Virtue: A New Translation of the Tao-te ching *of Laozi as Interpreted by Wang Bi*, tr. Richard John Lynn — 1999

The Four Hundred Songs of War and Wisdom: An Anthology of Poems from Classical Tamil, The Puranāṇūṟu, eds. and trans. George L. Hart and Hank Heifetz — 1999

Original Tao: Inward Training (Nei-yeh) and the Foundations of Taoist Mysticism, by Harold D. Roth — 1999

Lao Tzu's Tao Te Ching: A Translation of the Startling New Documents Found at Guodian, Robert G. Henricks — 2000

The Shorter Columbia Anthology of Traditional Chinese Literature, ed. Victor H. Mair — 2000

Mistress and Maid (Jiaohongji) by Meng Chengshun, tr. Cyril Birch — 2001

Chikamatsu: Five Late Plays, tr. and ed. C. Andrew Gerstle
The Essential Lotus: Selections from the Lotus Sutra, tr. Burton Watson 2002
Early Modern Japanese Literature: An Anthology, 1600–1900, ed. Haruo Shirane 2002

MODERN ASIAN LITERATURE

Modern Japanese Drama: An Anthology, ed. and tr. Ted. Takaya. Also in paperback ed. 1979
Mask and Sword: Two Plays for the Contemporary Japanese Theater, by Yamazaki Masakazu, tr. J. Thomas Rimer 1980
Yokomitsu Riichi, Modernist, Dennis Keene 1980
Nepali Visions, Nepali Dreams: The Poetry of Laxmiprasad Devkota, tr. David Rubin 1980
Literature of the Hundred Flowers, vol. 1: *Criticism and Polemics*, ed. Hualing Nieh 1981
Literature of the Hundred Flowers, vol. 2: *Poetry and Fiction*, ed. Hualing Nieh 1981
Modern Chinese Stories and Novellas, 1919 1949, ed. Joseph S. M. Lau, C. T. Hsia, and Leo Ou-fan Lee. Also in paperback ed. 1984
A View by the Sea, by Yasuoka Shōtarō, tr. Kären Wigen Lewis 1984
Other Worlds: Arishima Takeo and the Bounds of Modern Japanese Fiction, by Paul Anderer 1984
Selected Poems of Sō Chōngju, tr. with introduction by David R. McCann 1989
The Sting of Life: Four Contemporary Japanese Novelists, by Van C. Gessel 1989
Stories of Osaka Life, by Oda Sakunosuke, tr. Burton Watson 1990
The Bodhisattva, or Samantabhadra, by Ishikawa Jun, tr. with introduction by William Jefferson Tyler 1990
The Travels of Lao Ts'an, by Liu T'ieh-yün, tr. Harold Shadick. Morningside ed. 1990
Three Plays by Kōbō Abe, tr. with introduction by Donald Keene 1993
The Columbia Anthology of Modern Chinese Literature, ed. Joseph S. M. Lau and Howard Goldblatt 1995
Modern Japanese Tanka, ed. and tr. by Makoto Ueda 1996

Masaoka Shiki: Selected Poems, ed. and tr. by Burton
  Watson — 1997
*Writing Women in Modern China: An Anthology of
  Women's Literature from the Early Twentieth Century*, ed. and tr. by Amy D. Dooling and Kristina
  M. Torgeson — 1998
American Stories, by Nagai Kafū, tr. Mitsuko Iriye — 2000
The Paper Door and Other Stories, by Shiga Naoya,
  tr. Lane Dunlop — 2001
Grass for My Pillow, by Saiichi Maruya, tr. Dennis
  Keene — 2002

STUDIES IN ASIAN CULTURE

The Ōnin War: History of Its Origins and Background, with a Selective Translation of the Chronicle of Ōnin, by H. Paul Varley — 1967
Chinese Government in Ming Times: Seven Studies,
  ed. Charles O. Hucker — 1969
The Actors' Analects (Yakusha Rongo), ed. and tr. by
  Charles J. Dunn and Bungō Torigoe — 1969
Self and Society in Ming Thought, by Wm. Theodore
  de Bary and the Conference on Ming Thought.
  Also in paperback ed. — 1970
A History of Islamic Philosophy, by Majid Fakhry, 2d
  ed. — 1983
Phantasies of a Love Thief: The Caurapañcāśikā Attributed to Bilhaṇa, by Barbara Stoler Miller — 1971
Iqbal: Poet-Philosopher of Pakistan, ed. Hafeez Malik — 1971
The Golden Tradition: An Anthology of Urdu Poetry,
  ed. and tr. Ahmed Ali. Also in paperback ed. — 1973
*Conquerors and Confucians: Aspects of Political
  Change in Late Yüan China*, by John W. Dardess — 1973
The Unfolding of Neo-Confucianism, by Wm.
  Theodore de Bary and the Conference on Seventeenth-Century Chinese Thought. Also in paperback ed. — 1975
To Acquire Wisdom: The Way of Wang Yang-ming, by
  Julia Ching — 1976
Gods, Priests, and Warriors: The Bhṛgus of the Mahābhārata, by Robert P. Goldman — 1977
*Mei Yao-ch'en and the Development of Early Sung
  Poetry*, by Jonathan Chaves — 1976

The Legend of Semimaru, Blind Musician of Japan,
   by Susan Matisoff   1977
*Sir Sayyid Ahmad Khan and Muslim Modernization
   in India and Pakistan,* by Hafeez Malik   1980
The Khilafat Movement: Religious Symbolism and Political Mobilization in India, by Gail Minault   1982
The World of K'ung Shang-jen: A Man of Letters in Early Ch'ing China, by Richard Strassberg   1983
The Lotus Boat: The Origins of Chinese Tz'u Poetry in T'ang Popular Culture, by Marsha L. Wagner   1984
Expressions of Self in Chinese Literature, ed. Robert E. Hegel and Richard C. Hessney   1985
Songs for the Bride: Women's Voices and Wedding Rites of Rural India, by W. G. Archer; eds. Barbara Stoler Miller and Mildred Archer   1986
The Confucian Kingship in Korea: Yŏngjo and the Politics of Sagacity, by JaHyun Kim Haboush   1988

COMPANIONS TO ASIAN STUDIES

Approaches to the Oriental Classics, ed. Wm. Theodore de Bary   1959
Early Chinese Literature, by Burton Watson. Also in paperback ed.   1962
Approaches to Asian Civilizations, eds. Wm. Theodore de Bary and Ainslie T. Embree   1964
The Classic Chinese Novel: A Critical Introduction, by C. T. Hsia. Also in paperback ed.   1968
Chinese Lyricism: Shih Poetry from the Second to the Twelfth Century, tr. Burton Watson. Also in paperback ed.   1971
A Syllabus of Indian Civilization, by Leonard A. Gordon and Barbara Stoler Miller   1971
Twentieth-Century Chinese Stories, ed. C. T. Hsia and Joseph S. M. Lau. Also in paperback ed. 1971
A Syllabus of Chinese Civilization, by J. Mason Gentzler, 2d ed.   1972
A Syllabus of Japanese Civilization, by H. Paul Varley, 2d ed.   1972
An Introduction to Chinese Civilization, ed. John Meskill, with the assistance of J. Mason Gentzler   1973
An Introduction to Japanese Civilization, ed. Arthur E. Tiedemann   1974

Ukifune: Love in the Tale of Genji, ed. Andrew Pekarik   1982
The Pleasures of Japanese Literature, by Donald Keene   1988
A Guide to Oriental Classics, eds. Wm. Theodore de Bary and Ainslie T. Embree; 3d edition ed. Amy Vladeck Heinrich, 2 vols.   1989

INTRODUCTION TO ASIAN CIVILIZATIONS
Wm. Theodore de Bary, General Editor

Sources of Japanese Tradition, 1958; paperback ed., 2 vols., 1964. 2d ed., vol. 1, 2001, compiled by Wm. Theodore de Bary, Donald Keene, George Tanabe, and Paul Varley

Sources of Indian Tradition, 1958; paperback ed., 2 vols., 1964. 2d ed., 2 vols.,   1988

Sources of Chinese Tradition, 1960, paperback ed., 2 vols., 1964. 2d ed., vol. 1, 1999, compiled by Wm. Theodore de Bary and Irene Bloom; vol. 2, 2000, compiled by Wm. Theodore de Bary and Richard Lufrano

Sources of Korean Tradition, 1997; 2 vols., vol. 1, 1997, compiled by Peter H. Lee and Wm. Theodore de Bary; vol. 2, 2001, compiled by Yŏngho Ch'oe, Peter H. Lee, and Wm. Theodore de Bary

NEO-CONFUCIAN STUDIES

Instructions for Practical Living and Other Neo-Confucian Writings by Wang Yang-ming, tr. Wing-tsit Chan   1963
Reflections on Things at Hand: The Neo-Confucian Anthology, comp. Chu Hsi and Lü Tsu-ch'ien, tr. Wing-tsit Chan   1967
Self and Society in Ming Thought, by Wm. Theodore de Bary and the Conference on Ming Thought. Also in paperback ed.   1970
The Unfolding of Neo-Confucianism, by Wm. Theodore de Bary and the Conference on Seventeenth-Century Chinese Thought. Also in paperback ed.   1975
Principle and Practicality: Essays in Neo-Confucianism and Practical Learning, eds. Wm.

Theodore de Bary and Irene Bloom. Also in paperback ed. 1979
The Syncretic Religion of Lin Chao-en, by Judith A. Berling 1980
The Renewal of Buddhism in China: Chu-hung and the Late Ming Synthesis, by Chün-fang Yü 1981
Neo-Confucian Orthodoxy and the Learning of the Mind-and-Heart, by Wm. Theodore de Bary 1981
Yüan Thought: Chinese Thought and Religion Under the Mongols, eds. Hok-lam Chan and Wm. Theodore de Bary 1982
The Liberal Tradition in China, by Wm. Theodore de Bary 1983
The Development and Decline of Chinese Cosmology, by John B. Henderson 1984
The Rise of Neo-Confucianism in Korea, by Wm. Theodore de Bary and JaHyun Kim Haboush 1985
Chiao Hung and the Restructuring of Neo-Confucianism in Late Ming, by Edward T. Ch'ien 1985
Neo-Confucian Terms Explained: Pei-hsi tzu-i, by Ch'en Ch'un, ed. and trans. Wing-tsit Chan 1986
Knowledge Painfully Acquired: K'un-chih chi, by Lo Ch'in-shun, ed. and trans. Irene Bloom 1987
To Become a Sage: The Ten Diagrams on Sage Learning, by Yi T'oegye, ed. and trans. Michael C. Kalton 1988
The Message of the Mind in Neo-Confucian Thought, by Wm. Theodore de Bary 1989

GPSR Authorized Representative: Easy Access System Europe, Mustamäe tee 50, 10621 Tallinn, Estonia, gpsr.requests@easproject.com

www.ingramcontent.com/pod-product-compliance
Lightning Source LLC
Chambersburg PA
CBHW050859300426
44111CB00010B/1302